Waltzing at the Window
Dancing in the Delight of Prayer

By Sharon Riddle

*The testing of any principle of prayer
is found in the journals of those who take it to heart.*

Copyright © 2005 by Sharon Riddle
Waltzing at the Window
By Sharon Riddle

Printed in the United States of America
ISBN 0-9761583-4-5
All rights reserved.
No part of this publication may be reproduced or transmitted in any form or by any means without written permission of the publisher.

Unless otherwise indicated, Scripture taken from the *New American Standard Bible*, Copyright © 1960, 1962, 1963, 1968, 1971, 1972, 1973, 1975, 1977, 1995 by The Lockman Foundation. Used by permission.

Olive Leaf Publications
www.OliveLeafPublications.com
Olive Leaf Publication books are distributed through Lightning Source, Inc. and Ingram Books.

Acknowledgments

My thanks
- To the Lord: without You I am nothing.
- To Terry, Sally and Jean for their editorial abilities. The Lord knows how much I need and value your help. I hope your crowns have double rubies!
- To the Olive Branch Church for their love and support during the difficult days in God's waiting room. Thank you for your prayers. They are God's best gift to us.
- To Beth for being my ministry assistant and helping tackle the tasks of each day.
- To Mary for mowing the lawn and cleaning the house so I could spend time helping others.
- To Ike for all the times you opened a can of chicken noodle soup so I could keep working.

Jesus answered and said, "A man can receive nothing unless it has been given him from Heaven." John 1:27

My teaching is not mine, but His who sent me. John 7:16b

But as for me, the nearness of God is my good; I have made the Lord God my refuge, that I may tell of all Thy works. Psalm 73:28

Table of Contents

Acknowledgments 3
Introduction 7
A Time to Dance 11
Dancing in Famine – Naomi 21
Dancing in Conflict – Daniel 41
Dancing on the Water – Peter 57
Dancing in the Fire – Shadrach, Meshach, Abed-nego 69
Dancing in Besiegement – King Ahab 85
Dancing in Victory – Joshua 107
Dancing in Thanksgiving - Jehosaphat and David 119
Conclusion 133

Introduction

This book is about what I call the dance of prayer. It is a book that encompasses the high steps of praise and the low bowing response of a servant. It is a moment by moment song of trust with heart-responses as its rhythm. It is not prayer 101, but 501, a graduate course that ushers us onto a lifetime of learning.

In our first stages of prayer we must overcome the enemy's primitive deceptions. Satan wants us to believe that prayer is boring and difficult. When the Lord proves to us that it is exciting and simple, we move on to new ground. But then the enemy tries to deceive us into believing that our prayers are ineffective and that we are unworthy. When we learn that they are precise weapons and that we are utterly dependent on Him for our worth, our opponent must try new things to trip us up. He wants us to smack into impenetrable barriers time and time again, which cause us to become discouraged as we are trapped by our lack of understanding. He wants us to sway back and forth near the punch bowl as the hour grows late and become content, thinking that we are truly dancing. Or he is happy when we venture out onto the floor alone, completely helpless and pitifully left to our own inadequate resources. But the sheer joy of the dance, of hearing His voice request our presence to dance in partnership with Him, can become our greatest treasure. When coupled with the shoes of obedience and the eyes of faith, it surpasses all of earth's treasures.

You are truly "waltzing" at the window of prayer when you realize that 1) without His partnership you have no dance at all, and 2) without His power you have no skill to your step, and 3) without His leadings you are earthbound, a stumbling prisoner chained to imperfections.

But when you begin to feel His pressings—His urgings—and you follow them more than your own human designs you will experience a dance that is extraordinary. The Holy Spirit is a "heavenly Fred Astaire" who can lead you through His Word to tiptoe on the ceiling as easily as He can on the floor. He can guide you through difficulties and around impossible obstacles if your will is released into His.

The dance of God and man is peculiar. We can <u>never</u> predict His next movement—no matter how long we have been His partner. His dips and twirls are spontaneous and exhilarating. He often leaves the boundaries of the dance floor to whisk us through the garden full of sweet-smelling, blossoming things—and onto hillsides that provide a marvelous view and a new perspective. The path that takes us there may be full of thorns, briars and pain. To continue the dance, we must crawl at times.

To learn to waltz we will peer into the lives of those in Scripture who have accepted God's invitation to the dance floor. We will observe people who have obediently walked with God over many years, who have experienced great trials, and who have continually made prayer the cornerstone of their existence.

There is no quick way to learn "the dance," for time varies between each step. We must learn to wait on Him for each move. We must become accustomed to the silence of the music while He is preparing His next impulse. We must not assume that He has left the floor, that He is still, or that He has abandoned us even though we may not feel or see His motion.

It is my fervent prayer that we will together decide today to go beyond dancing 101 and those painted patterns of shoeprints on the floor, leave behind the stilted movements of regulated quiet time patterns, and finally, listen for His invitation to the floor and begin to really experience "the dance" as it was intended.

1

A TIME TO DANCE

Our adventure is prayer, and by illustration, dancing. By the way, do you dance? You can learn much about the former through studying the latter. I grew up in a family that didn't dance. We didn't do it because 1) the places where dancing was allowed weren't conducive to the Christian life, 2) dancing encouraged a man to dance with someone other than his wife, and 3) because of the sinful urges that dancing sometimes causes. But when I refer to <u>Waltzing at the Window</u>, I am not referring to dancing in this respect. I am talking about the natural and free response of a child to hear rhythm and begin to sway. There is a dance that is born within us and it is either encouraged or choked early on.

My friend, Lydia, is a worship dancer. As a young girl, oddly enough, she was very clumsy. Her family made jokes about this and she had to get used to being called "the klutz." When she came to the Lord, He began to deal with the hurts and the hindrances. She found that during her quiet times with the Lord, He began to invite her to release herself into His hands physically and emotionally as well as spiritually. Dance became a regular part of her quiet time and the Lord began opening opportunities for her to use this gift in front of others. Now, if you saw her dance you wouldn't believe that she was ever a clumsy teenager. She is a woman submitted to God and completely responsive to His "touch."

Why must we be able to "dance" in our prayers? I am speaking symbolically here. There are just times when nothing else is an adequate response. Think of the day when the Lord parted the Red Sea for the Israelites. How would it have been if Miriam had turned to Moses and said, "Praise the Lord, Brother!" Would that have been sufficient praise for the God of the Universe who had held back the mighty waters and had used His breath to create a dry path through the waters? No! On the day that Lazarus was raised from the dead, would it have been enough to send a formal "thank you" card to Jesus for His provision that day? No! There are times when we MUST DANCE. The sheer miraculous work of God is too much for earthly words and steps. On our balcony of prayer (a closet just isn't big enough) we can enter the realm of the Heavenly where there is no pain, no pressure, no etiquette and no restraint to adore our Father, who is above all.

Perhaps you have experienced a few times in your life when one of your greatest answers to prayer came about unexpectantly and took your breath away. If you have read my first two books then you know I have experienced some marvelous answers to prayer, which have made me dance with delight. I am still praying for a friend of mine to come to the Lord. I guarantee that when the call comes that he has finally given his heart to the Lord, I WILL DANCE IN THE STREETS. I will dance because of all the little prayers I have prayed over his life, and all the times his family and I have pressed God for a lifeline for him. I will dance because I will know that my prayers moved the hand of God as well as the Rock of Gibraltar (my unsaved friend). Smile. I will dance because something that no man could do will be done in front of my eyes.

I will dance like the lame man danced when Jesus healed him through Peter and John in Acts chapter three. Can you imagine what that was like? A man who had been lame from birth, who had never even taken a step began to walk and leap and praise God. He went from lameness to dancing in a matter of a moment. That is the kind of dancing I am talking about. That is the kind of praying I am teaching about. In order to dance without ever walking you must have the touch of God on your life. There is a response of faith and submission that each of us lame men must bring to the table. But in God's hands we can all rise up from sin-sick beds and learn to "leap."

Can you imagine the dancing in the streets of Persia when after three days of fasting the tables were turned on Haman, the enemy of the Jews? The very plot that was meant to annihilate them, turned to prosper them. You are really <u>Waltzing at the Window</u> when you learn to celebrate the plunder while you are watching others build your gallows.

David understood that his dance was for the Lord and not for other people. It was possible for them to misunderstand the unabashed response of praise and adoration, as did his wife Michal. David, however, was willing to relinquish self-focus to offer the Lord the wholehearted response He deserved.

As the ark of the Lord was entering the City of David, Michal daughter of Saul watched from a window. And when she saw King David leaping and dancing before the Lord, she despised him in her heart. 2 Samuel 6:16

If we can identify the things that keep us from that kind of free response to the Lord, we will be able to see what changes need to take place in order to grow in our prayer lives. What keeps <u>you</u>

from dancing? Our traditions sometimes keep us in our place on the sidelines, only able to watch the beauty taking place on the floor. There are other times that our teachings trip us up and keep us from the marvelous partnership God wants us to experience in our praying. What limitations have been put on your prayer life because of the inadequate training of those who mentored you? Ask the Lord to remove the crutches and braces from your belief system so that you can learn to soar with Him.

We have to admit, though, that it is not just the fault of other generations that hold us back. Our pride can be an important hindrance also. Keeping an eye on the crowd keeps our eyes from meeting His and enjoying a oneness with Him. Because of pride a person may despise or be embarrassed by another's zeal. Remember Mary's unreserved show of affection when she poured out the perfume and washed Jesus' feet with her tears, as recorded in Luke 7:26? "Why this waste?" You'll hear the same thing when you devote time to prayer and turn aside in the midst of chaos to honor Him.

To move to a new place of prayer you need to release yourself and become vulnerable in the Master's hands. I do not mean in any way, shape or form that we should give in to bizarre impulses of random and unbiblical behavior in our prayer. These have become commonplace in our generation. Rather, I mean that we should embrace Him fully and forget our limitations as a result of the beautiful partnership we experience. We should be willing to accept the unexpected as normal.

We are in the midst right now of constructing an educational building on our church property. It will house classrooms and a worship center for our children's ministry. I recently overheard someone asking our builder if the project would be completed by the beginning of the school year. Tony, our builder, asked what that date was. When told it was the Tuesday after Labor Day, he replied that that wouldn't be a very reasonable expectation. I smiled to myself as I thought how we have come to expect very unreasonable things around here because God is God and sometimes He has unreasonable expectations. He also has the means to accomplish them. (Just a note here: the building wasn't completed until December 2005, but my faith was there in case He wanted it done sooner. Smile.)

And the rabble who were among them had greedy desires; and also the sons of Israel wept again and said, "Who will give us meat to eat? We remember the fish which we used to eat free in Egypt, the cucumbers and the melons and the leeks and the onions and the garlic, but now our appetite is gone. There is nothing at all to look at except this manna." Now the manna was like coriander seed, and its appearance like that of bdellium. The people would go about and gather it and grind it between two millstones or beat it in the mortar, and boil it in the pot and make cakes with it; and its taste was as the taste of cakes baked with oil. And when the dew fell on the camp at night, the manna would fall with it. Now Moses heard the people weeping throughout their families, each man at the doorway of his tent; and the anger of the Lord was kindled greatly, and Moses was displeased. So Moses said to the Lord, "Why hast Thou been so hard on Thy servant? And why have I not found favor in Thy sight, that Thou hast laid the burden of all this people on me? Was it I who conceived all this people? Was it I who brought them forth, that Thou shouldest say to me, 'Carry them in your bosom as a nurse carries a nursing infant, to the land which Thou didst swear to their fathers'? Where am I to get meat to give to all this people? For they weep before me, saying, 'Give us meat that we may eat!' I alone am not able to carry all this people, because it is too burdensome for me. So if Thou art going to deal thus with me, please kill me at once, if I have found favor in Thy sight, and do not let me see my wretchedness." Numbers 11:4-15

I have been meditating lately in Numbers 11, where the Israelites complain about NO MEAT. God assures Moses that not only will they get meat, but that they will eat it for an entire month until it comes out their noses and until they are sick of it. Moses tries to visualize what God has just declared. "But Lord," he says, "there are over six hundred thousand of us on foot." My husband says he was referring to the number of men that had been counted at this point in the journey. Moses goes on to say that even if all the fish in the sea were served up, it wouldn't be enough, that if entire flocks were slaughtered, it couldn't possibly be enough to feed this many people for a month. Here is one of our problems: we can't always see HOW God is going to do what He says. It is beyond our comprehension to figure out the practical means He will use to actually do the thing He has said He would do. But we know enough about God to know this: if He said it, He will do it.

Say to the people, "Consecrate yourselves for tomorrow, and you shall eat meat; for you have wept in the ears of the Lord, saying, 'Oh that someone would give us meat to eat! For we were well-off in Egypt.' Therefore the Lord will give you meat and you shall eat. You shall eat, not one day, nor two days, nor five days, nor ten days, nor twenty days, but a whole month, until it comes out of your nostrils and becomes loathsome to you; because you have rejected the Lord who is among you and have wept before Him, saying, 'Why did we ever leave Egypt?'" Numbers 11:18-20

God proceeded to send a wind, which indeed blew in enough quail to accomplish His purposes. Even the one who gathered the least of the quail gathered ten homers. A homer is a heap, which is about eight bushels. The ones who collected the least brought in at least eighty bushels of meat! I was thinking about this passage one morning in my prayer time when the Lord brought this next verse to mind:

For behold, He who forms mountains and creates the wind and declares to man what are His thoughts, He who makes dawn into darkness and treads on the high places of the earth, The Lord God of hosts is His name. Amos 4:13

    I'm a cook and every once in awhile I get into my "workshop" and make something. I have at my disposal the desire, the tools and the ingredients. I create cookies or a casserole or something. But when God goes into His workshop, He creates "mountains." He forms "wind." When we hear His unmistakable voice proclaim that He is going to provide meat or buildings or salvations or healings, we can just smile and head out onto the dance floor of praise in anticipation.

    In my other two books I mentioned that we have been praying about my husband's health for about six years. Ever since he returned from a mission trip to the Philippines, his health has rapidly declined. We now know that he came home infected with a couple of parasites, but it took the doctors a long time to discover the problem. They diagnosed one parasite a year after the trip, and the other parasite two years after the trip. Then two years later he was diagnosed with fibromyalgia and began to have shooting pains throughout his arms and legs. These kept him awake during most of the night. We made a lot of trips to different doctors. They increased his pain medication often, but it didn't seem to be doing much good. We began to wonder if he would even be able to continue in ministry. What was the Lord doing?

    One Sunday Ike had trouble staying awake in his morning prayer time with the elders and others who came to pray. He also had a lot of trouble with his morning message in the first service. He lost his place a couple of times and had a very dry mouth. We found out later that he had been taking two different medications that were in conflict with each other. They were basically frying his brain. We ended up taking him to the emergency room after the first service because he felt so awful. That painful morning God did something wonderful. He prompted a lady named Karen to get our church praying for Ike twenty-four hours a day, seven days a week. Our friend Marilyn made a little poster where people could to commit to pray for Ike around the clock; people started filling it up with their signatures, and in turn, the bowls of Heaven with their prayers. Many people had already been praying, some on a daily basis. But here was an all-out attack on this affliction, which was affecting an entire church body.

It must also be noted that during this time two friends (Joyce and Diana) made time to come and pray specifically over Ike. Many had done this over the past six years, but because of the timing, I must include it.

Not long after this we met with his regular physician. During our discussion over Ike's health the Lord allowed this doctor to see our deep commitment to ministry and our desire not to shame His name or His work. It touched him deeply and he began to investigate my husband's case with even more vigor.

A couple of weeks later he called with some important news. He had attended a conference that week on the endocrine system. He had looked over Ike's records again and had found that every single one of his hormones were below the minimum functioning level. After more tests and shots it was determined that Ike needed some hormone replacement therapy. Around the same time, another doctor Ike had seen realized that he was severely deficient in vitamin D. Quickly he authorized huge doses and requested that Ike sit in the sun for twenty minutes each day. The next Sunday as I watched my husband preach with new vigor, I wanted to dance. I did so in my heart. We are still in the midst of this scenario and it is too early to see the outcome of the entire trial. But I have learned much already through the journey.

(Just a note: after this brief period of improvement, Ike's health has continued to decline, but we know that it has only been through the prayers of His people that the Lord has sustained him and helped him through the past year.)

When God goes into His workshop He is capable of creating DNA, H_2O and atomic energy. So, if He proclaims that there will be meat in the wilderness or water from a rock, I must give up the notion that I am ever going to be able to figure out HOW He will do it. I also need to put away the thought that I can figure out WHEN He will do it, or even WHY. But in the darkest of nights we can all hold onto His words, knowing that if He said it, He can do it. We can run out into the streets and dance the dance of Miriam while soldiers and chariots are running towards us with destruction in their hands, because we worship the GREAT I AM.

Over what difficulty are you praying right now? Are you in the midst of a dark day? Put on your dancing shoes and praise Him for His excellent greatness. Praise Him for His ability to create worlds. Praise Him for His ability to bring order to *your* world. Begin your dance of delight while it is still night. Leap on the seashore before you ever see a miracle morning emerge with the sunrise.

Prayer Journal entry:
In 1999, I begin praying for a young man named Rodney who feels the Lord might be calling him into the ministry. Soon after he shares this with me, he disappears from our church. I continue praying for him.
I see Rodney in 2005. He has been attending a different church during these past years and just preached his first sermon. He is on fire for the Lord. Praise the Lord!

Prayer Journal entry:
1/15/05 Talked with my cousin Janet. In July my mother's only sister will be celebrating her 90th birthday. I ask the Lord if I can go and visit her.
6/5/05 The Lord provides all the resources to go and spend several days with my Aunt Alice. We have a wonderful time of fellowship and I thank the Lord for answering my heart's desire prayer.

Prayer Journal entry:
In September of 2001 I think of the title of a children's story that I want to write. I put the story in my journal and begin to pray over it.
1/30/05 The Lord gave me "the hook" for the story: Princess Batilda can't say, "I'm sorry."
2/21/05 Made some progress on writing the story.
9/23/05 Asked the Lord for more help on the story.
10/11/05 Progress is given on the story.
10/14/05 The story is completely finished in one session. My friend Marilyn is working on illustrating it. Praise the Lord!

2

DANCING IN FAMINE

Naomi was a survivor. She had survived a famine. (Some people who survived *The Great Depression* testified that after you go through something that horrific you are never the same again.) Naomi had also survived a move away from the place that she loved. Some of you know what that's like. You have left a comfortable place where you were known and loved and headed out to places with names you couldn't even pronounce, places full of people whose customs were very strange and different from what you have known. In addition to that Naomi had survived the death of a spouse. Some of you know what that is all about. You've made their dreams your dreams, met their needs as if they were your own, poured your life into theirs, but now you have to walk a path of your own. You may be a survivor too. Naomi also survived a slow death as she watched her sons marry pagan women. She survived dealing with the guilt of what she could have done differently, what she should have done differently in raising them. She must have been familiar with God's instructions to the Israelites regarding intermarriage with pagans:

Furthermore, you shall not intermarry with them; you shall not give your daughters to their sons, nor shall you take their daughters for your sons. Deuteronomy 7:3

For if you ever go back and cling to the rest of these nations, these which remain among you, and intermarry with them, so that you associate with them and they with you, know with certainty that the Lord your God will not continue to drive these nations out from before you; **but they shall be a snare and a trap to you, and a whip on your sides and thorns in your eyes,** *until you perish from off this good land which the Lord your God has given you. Joshua 23:12-13*

Some of you know how painful it can be to watch your children make choices against the will of God. You have prayed for your children and their families. Some of them may be walking with the Lord and some may not be. You are survivors in this respect as well.

Naomi had survived an environment full of spiritual famine. She was living among pagans. She was attempting to make an impact on them, but sometimes their ways had filtered into her life. Her spiritual solutions didn't always seem to be working, but she had survived.

She had survived ten years of unanswered prayers. What might have been on Naomi's prayer list? To have a happy family with grandchildren, plenty of food, to be restored to her country, her friends, and her extended family, to make an impact on those around her…she might have prayed over this list day after day, but she had not seen one of those prayers answered for at least a decade. Have you ever been asked by the Lord to intercede for things that require years of prayer? Some of us may never have the experience of coming day by day and laboring in prayer, like in childbirth, over something like the need for revival, and have to mark off the decades without seeing a fulfillment. But Naomi did.

She had survived the death of her two sons. She could remember the day she had brought them into the world. And now she knew what it was like to nail them and all the dreams she had had for their lives in wooden boxes. Mahlon and Chilion were gone. So were the moments of making them their favorite meal and hearing their accounts of the day, seeing their muddy footprints on her kitchen floor, and enjoying their hugs. Yet, life went on and Naomi had survived. But with each event something else had begun to die: Naomi's hope. It was lying it its own little coffin in the graveyard of her heart.

Naomi survived, but her hope died.

I met with a woman last week whose hope is dying. She is angry that her mother is dead. And now she thinks that everyone else in her life is the source of her unhappiness. She is just so sad and she doesn't know what to do with all the sadness. We shouldn't be too hard on her or on Naomi. We may have been through some of these things ourselves, but I doubt that any of us has been through all these things.

It was just easier to blame God than to deal with her own sadness. Ruth 1:21 gives us a window into her thinking: *"**I went out full, but the Lord has brought me back empty**. Why do you call me Naomi, since **the Lord has witnessed against me** and **the Almighty has afflicted me?**"* What is Naomi's limited thinking of "full?" What is her limited thinking of "empty-handed?" I went out "full" (of this world's treasures—money, husband, sons…) and came back empty (without any of them). The Lord's evaluation is that she went out "empty" and returned ready to be filled. Have you ever had your life emptied so that it could be filled? The recognition of our state of spiritual poverty makes us a prime candidate for blessing.

Hope is such a subtle thing that no one but the Lord knows if you have it or not. I have been noting the Lord's attention to our thoughts and see that this *to believe* or *not believe* muscle can be flexed or not flexed at any moment. Sarah didn't believe the angels when they said she would be pregnant in a year. But she did believe when she trusted her husband, even when he didn't make the right choices. God saw what was in her heart, and He honored her decision to believe in His power by writing her name in the Book of Hebrews' hall of faith.

So you can tell me everything's fine today, but God knows where you really are with Him. He can see in the midst of a mess if you trust Him, and he can see when your world looks like it's going fine if you are simply taking matters into your own hands.

In her heart she makes a decision to head HOME.

Then Naomi heard the news that God had visited His people (Ruth 6:1). The food that He had provided wasn't what caught her attention in my opinion. It was the thought of revival, **God's presence, His nearness**. And she began to long for it. So one quiet afternoon she decided to return to the spiritual life that she had known, but from which she had moved away. You also can make that choice today. You can turn back from the things that have stolen the time in His presence. You can hunger for revival more than lunch. And you can turn your attention to the Most High even if you, like Naomi, still have some questions about what's going on right now in your life.

You are here: the place on the map marked with the "X."

Have you ever been lost inside an unfamiliar mall? I have. It was an uncomfortable feeling. Fortunately, someone with a better perspective provided a map with reference points at different places. Thus, I was able to identify the exits, the restrooms, the different kinds of stores and, most importantly, *my* location clearly marked with a big "X." Right now Naomi is smack dab in the middle of a difficult trial. She is so near the end of her misery and so close to joy and gladness. We can see it, but she can't. Her circumstances are accomplishing a great deal in the bigger picture of God's plan, but she doesn't know it yet. Is this where you are right now? Are your hopes and dreams nailed down in caskets? Are you wondering, "Is God for me or against me?" Naomi wondered, "Where are the blessings of righteousness?" Are you wondering that same thing?

We, looking back on her life have the advantage of the big picture. We know the whole story. We see that God is caring for her in the midst of her trouble. God is using the heat of her circumstances to produce the fragrance of Him in a foreign land. But she can't see it. He is using trouble to introduce Himself to unbelievers. Who is being introduced to the living God through your pile of trouble? Who is enjoying the aroma of Christ through the difficult circumstances of your life today?

Naomi is ready to lie down and die in her sadness, but God is rising up in action to produce life and joy. He is working on a plan to change the world. He's working on the lineage of Messiah. God's working on His intricate plan for redeeming mankind and Naomi can't get past, "I'm empty."

<u>50 miles to Bethlehem and "revival"</u>

Naomi had heard about revival. Now she wanted to taste it. How far are you from revival? It starts with the smallest of actions. Naomi took that first step when she picked up her heart and her bags and headed home. What happened on the way? She had a profound mid-journey experience that caused Ruth to become a believer in God. Ruth's faith is so fresh and real and contagious. You can read about it in Ruth 1:16-17. Ruth said, *"Do not urge me to leave you or turn back from following you; for where you go, I will go, and where you lodge, I will lodge. Your people shall be my people, and your God, my God. Where you die, I will die, and there I will be buried. Thus may the Lord do to me, and worse, if anything but death parts you and me."* I believe that Ruth's commitment had a profound impact on Naomi. Sound familiar? God often uses the fresh zeal of a new believer to start up the fire in our own hearts again. In addition, one of Naomi's possible ten-year prayers has just been answered!

Getting back to the map in the mall... You look for where you want to be and for the right path to get there. Right choices bring blessing. The naysayer will try to convince you that following the Lord is a dead-end path, but God tells us: let none that wait on the Lord be ashamed. No matter where you start from, obedience will always take you to the right destination.

Let's take a look at God's map to see what's ahead for Naomi. A "daughter" who is better to her than seven sons. Redemption—Boaz acts as her kinsmen redeemer. Her soon to be new "son" Boaz will be a man of integrity who is deeply spiritual. (He blesses his workers with spiritual truth.) He was actually the son of Rahab who had risked her life to shelter the twelve spies. His father was Salmon, whom some scholars believe was one of the two spies Rahab had protected. She also gets a grandchild that she is privileged to nurse. This baby is so much her own personal blessing that her friends announce, "A son has been born to Naomi" and <u>they</u> get to name the baby. Soon she will have an abundance of food and resource for doing the will of God. She will be the recipient of much fame. After all, we're reading and talking about her today, thousands of years later. She will also receive honor for Naomi will become the great, great grandmother of King David. She can't see over the next ninety to one hundred years to know this will all be taking place. She will also get to experience full joy, the kind that only comes from having <u>all</u> your ten-year prayers answered.

God had all this planned for her life, but Naomi can't see what's around the bend. And hanging around her mall and yours is the enemy, Satan the deceiver. He knows what God has promised and his job is to try to get you off course. Satan is hanging around to see how he can "help" you work through your questions and doubts. He chimes in that God has forgotten you and that you are not going to make a difference. The journey is too hard. After all you've been praying these prayers for years now. There is no hope. God has good things planned for others, but not for you. There are days Naomi has let herself listen to his lies. There are days she even started to believe them.

Dr. Neil T. Anderson tells a little story in his book, <u>The Bondage Breaker</u>, that illustrates the enemy's role. When Neil was a young boy His father had to pay a visit to a neighbor's farm, and Neil and his brother rode along in the family pickup. That neighbor had a yapping dog that scared Neil so much he would end up on top of the pickup out of fear. Of course his wiser father and brother just stood their ground and the dog never bothered them. As soon as Neil discovered that the dog's power was in the fear he instilled, he learned to get down off the pickup. Dr. Anderson now tells people that Satan is like that yapping dog. He encourages people to get off the pickup and start living their lives by faith in the truth of what God has said.

<u>The Truth</u>

The truth about Naomi's life is that God is using her to influence Ruth's life. God is giving Naomi a relationship so that she can share the difficulties along life's road. You might think that I mean a relationship with Ruth, but I'm actually talking about a relationship with Him, up close and personal. This is the greatest treasure He can give. God has a plan to give Naomi the "family" she has always dreamed of—her heart's desire. And finally, God has a plan to honor Naomi.

The truth about you, if you are walking in obedience, is that God is using you to win hearts and lives right now. God is giving you the chance to share the road with himself, up close and personal—or distantly. It's your choice. God is preparing our heart's desires. God has a plan to honor our obedience.

We can't really pinpoint when Naomi began to hope again. It might have been when she started praying little prayers over her daughters-in-law on the road, or maybe when she reached Jerusalem and prayed over Ruth for God's favor as she gleaned in Boaz's field, but God knows the very moment it occurred. He knows when you're trusting and when you're not. This is a critical decision: to believe.

We read about the potential in Hebrews 11:33-34: *ho **by faith** conquered kingdoms, performed acts of righteousness, **obtained promises**, shut the mouths of lions, quenched the power of fire, escaped the edge of the sword, from weakness were made strong, became mighty in war, put foreign armies to flight.*

And without becoming weak in faith he contemplated his own body, now as good as dead since he was about a hundred years old, and the deadness of Sarah's womb; yet, with respect to the promise of God, he did not waver in unbelief, but grew strong in faith, giving glory to God, and being fully assured that what He had promised, He was able also to perform. Romans 4:19-21

You might be facing some impossible circumstances today, but you can make a critical, life-changing decision if you choose to believe God and His Word in the midst of your circumstances.

And God is able to make all grace abound to you, that always having all sufficiency in everything, you may have an abundance for every good deed. 2 Corinthians 9:8

But they who seek the Lord shall not be in want of any good thing. Psalm 34:10b

Give, and it will be given to you; good measure, pressed down, shaken together, running over, they will pour into your lap. For by your standard of measure it will be measured to you in return. Luke 6:38

For the Lord God is a sun and shield; The Lord gives grace and glory; no good thing does He withhold from those who walk uprightly. Psalm 84:11

...Seeing that His divine power has granted to us everything pertaining to life and godliness, through the true knowledge of Him who called us by His own glory and excellence. For by these He has granted to us His precious and magnificent promises, in order that by them you might become partakers of the divine nature, having escaped the corruption that is in the world by lust. 2 Peter 1:3-4

And he said to him, 'My child, you have always been with me, and all that is mine is yours.' Luke 15:31

A good man leaves an inheritance to his children's children, and the wealth of the sinner is stored up for the righteous. Proverbs 13:22

For to a person who is good in His sight He has given wisdom and knowledge and joy, while to the sinner He has given the task of gathering and collecting so that he may give to one who is good in God's sight. This too is vanity and striving after wind. Ecclesiastes 2:26

Indeed, none of those who wait for Thee will be ashamed. Psalm 25:3s

It doesn't matter where you are right now. Whenever you are walking with God and your faith muscle is flexing, you are on the road to blessing, fruitfulness and joy: they are surely up ahead. Faith has no backup plan. It's putting all your eggs in God's basket. You are here today (where the "X" is), but you don't have to be here tomorrow. You can make a choice to head for the place of God's presence and to put your trust in Him and His Word. You might not have the whole map, but He does and you can put your trust in His Word. It's enough to get us walking each morning on the journey.

Know therefore that the Lord your God, He is God, the faithful God, who keeps His covenant and His lovingkindness to a **thousandth generation with those who love Him and keep His** *commandments. Deuteronomy 7:9*

God says in Deuteronomy 7:9 that the right choices we make today affect one thousand generations that follow us. He kept His promise even to Rahab, a pagan harlot, and He will surely keep His promise to you also. Get off the pickup and start listening to the Lord's voice. He has a good report within your circumstances. What did He say when His people were about to enter the Promised Land? I will go with you. I will help you. When you feel that your hope is dying, head home to the Father's presence. Meet Him on the road. He'll help you. He has a huge plan for your life. Is your faith muscle flexing? If so, the revival has already started. You can sing Habakkuk's worship song:

Though the fig tree should not blossom, and there be no fruit on the vines, Though the yield of the olive should fail, and the fields produce no food, though the flock should be cut off from the fold, and there be no cattle in the stalls, yet I will exult in the Lord, I will rejoice in the God of my salvation. The Lord God is my strength; and He has made my feet like hinds' feet, and makes me walk on my high places. Habakkuk 3:17-19

Or consider the modern meditation of this theme as sung by Matt Redman on his album, *Where Angels Fear to Tread* (2002) Used by permission.

Blessed Be Your Name

Blessed be Your name
In the land that is plentiful
Where Your streams of abundance flow
Blessed be Your name

Blessed be Your name
When I'm found in the desert place
Though I walk through the wilderness
Blessed be Your name

Every blessing You pour out
I'll turn back to praise
When the darkness closes in, Lord
Still I will say

Blessed be the name of the Lord
Blessed be Your name
Blessed be the name of the Lord
Blessed be Your glorious name

Blessed be Your name

When the sun's shining down on me
When the world's 'all as it should be'
Blessed be Your name

Blessed be Your name
On the road marked with suffering
Though there's pain in the offering
Blessed be Your name

Every blessing You pour out
I'll turn back to praise
When the darkness closes in, Lord
Still I will say

Blessed be the name of the Lord
Blessed be Your name
Blessed be the name of the Lord
Blessed be Your glorious name

You give and take away
You give and take away
My heart will choose to say
Lord, blessed be Your name

      In the midst of famine you can enjoy a feast of His presence. Like Micah you can look into the future and say confidently:

But as for me, I will watch expectantly for the Lord; I will wait for the God of my salvation. My God will hear me. Do not rejoice over me, O my enemy. Though I fall I will rise; though I dwell in darkness, the Lord is a light for me. Micah 7:7-8

Prayer Journal entry:
2/6/05 I hear that our school might not have eighth grade next year. This is the grade my daughter Beth will be in. I believe that it is just a stepping-stone to grow our faith and that it won't really happen. But I bring it before the Lord in my prayer time.

2/9/05 We get official word that there will be no eighth grade next year at our school. The class has been small and with several of the students on scholarship, it cannot support itself. We are also cramped in our facilities. We don't even know where we would put the class.

Here are some of my honest thoughts. I share them here because they remind me of Naomi. *I am disappointed—where is our faith? I am scared—what will we do with Beth?* I ask the Lord to show us what to do. He begins over the next few weeks to give me several verses that serve to guide us into the option of home schooling. Here are the verses the Lord used in the process:

Verses for Beth's 8th Grade Home Schooling

Purpose statement: *"**Remember this, and be assured; recall it to mind**, you transgressors. Remember the former things long past, for I am God, and there is no other; I am God, and there is no one like Me, **declaring the end from the beginning** and from ancient times things which have not been done, saying, 'My purpose will be established, and I will accomplish all My good pleasure;' calling a bird of prey from the east, the man of My purpose from a far country. Truly I have spoken; truly I will bring it to pass. I have planned it, **surely I will do it**."* Isaiah 46:8-11

- *Not to us, O Lord, not to us, but to Thy name give glory because of Thy loving-kindness, because of Thy truth. Why should the nations say, "Where, **now**, is their God?" But our God is in the heavens; He does whatever He pleases. Psalm 115:1-3*

- *God is not a man, that He should lie, nor a son of man, that He should repent; has He said, and will He not do it? Or has He spoken, and will He not make it good? Behold, I have received a command to bless; when He has blessed, then I cannot revoke it. He has not observed misfortune in Jacob; nor has He seen trouble in Israel; the Lord his God is with him, and the shout of a king is among them. God brings them out of Egypt, He is for them like the horns of the wild ox. Numbers 23:19-22*
- <u>***The Lord has been mindful of us; He will bless us***</u>*; He will bless the house of Israel; He will bless the house of Aaron. Psalm 115:12*
- *May the Lord **give you increase**, you and your children. Psalm 115:14*
- *And that you may tell **in the hearing of your son, and of your grandson**, how I made **a mockery of the Egyptians**, and how I performed My signs among them; that you may know that I am the Lord. Exodus 10:2*
- *And all the inhabitants of the earth are accounted as nothing, But **He does according to His will in the host of heaven** and among the inhabitants of earth; and **no one can ward off His hand** or say to Him, **"What hast Thou done?"** Daniel 4:35*
- *Do not fear, for I am with you; do not anxiously look about you, for I am your God. **I will strengthen you, surely I will help you**, surely I will uphold you with My righteous right hand. Behold all those who are angered at you will be shamed and dishonored; those who contend with you will be as nothing, and will perish. You will seek those who quarrel with you, but will not find them, those who war with you will be as nothing, and non-existent. For I am the Lord your God,*

who upholds your right hand, who says to you, "Do not fear, I will help you." Isaiah 41:10-13

- *Though Balak were to give me his house full of silver and gold, I could not do anything contrary to the command of the Lord,* **either good or bad, of my own accord***. What the Lord speaks, that I will speak. Numbers 24:13*

- *The Lord is near to all who call upon Him, to all who call upon Him in truth.* **He will fulfill the desire of those who fear Him; He will also hear their cry and will save them.** *Psalm 145:18-19*

- *I will instruct you and teach you in the way which you should go;* **I will counsel you with My eye upon you***. Psalm 32:8*

- *No man will be able to stand before you all the days of your life.* **Just as I have been with Moses, I will be with you; I will not fail you or forsake you.** *Be strong and courageous, for you shall give this people possession of the land which I swore to their fathers to give them.* **Only be strong and very courageous; be careful to do according to all the law which Moses My servant commanded you; do not turn from it to the right or to the left, so that you may have success wherever you go.** *Joshua 1:5-7*

- *My sheep hear My voice, and I know them, and* **they follow Me***. John 10:27*

- **Now faith is the assurance of things hoped for, the conviction of things not seen.** *For by it the men of old gained approval. By faith Moses, when he was born, was hidden for three months by his parents, because they saw he was a beautiful child; and* <u>**they were not afraid**</u> *of the king's edict. Hebrews 11:1-2,23*

- *The enemy said, "I will pursue, I will overtake, I will divide the spoil; my desire shall be gratified against them; I will draw out my sword, my hand shall destroy them." Thou didst blow with Thy wind, the sea covered them; they sank like lead in the mighty waters. Who is like Thee among the gods, O Lord? Who is like Thee, majestic in holiness, Awesome in praises,* **working wonders**? *In Thy lovingkindness Thou hast led the people whom Thou hast redeemed; in Thy strength Thou hast guided them to Thy holy habitation. Exodus 15:9-11,13*

- *Behold, I have received a command to bless; when He has blessed, then I cannot revoke it.* **He has not observed misfortune in Jacob; nor has He seen trouble in Israel; the Lord his God is with him,** *and the shout of a king is among them. God brings them out of Egypt,* **He is for them like the horns of the wild ox.** *Numbers 23:20-22*

- *Then their offspring will be known among the nations, and their descendants in the midst of the peoples. All who see them will recognize them because* **they are the offspring whom the Lord has blessed.** *Isaiah 61:9*

- *Ah Lord God! Behold, Thou hast made the heavens and the earth by Thy great power and by Thine outstretched arm!* **Nothing is too difficult for Thee, who showest lovingkindness to thousands,** *but repayest the iniquity of fathers into the bosom of their children after them, O great and mighty God. The Lord of hosts is His name; great in counsel and mighty in deed, whose eyes are open to all the ways of the sons of men, giving to everyone according to his ways and according to the fruit of his deed. Jeremiah 32:17-19*

- *And Jesus came up and spoke to them, saying,* **"All authority has been given to Me in heaven and on earth.** *Go therefore and make disciples of all the nations, baptizing them in the name of the Father and the Son and the Holy Spirit,* **teaching them to observe all that I commanded you; and lo, I am**

with you always, even to the end of the age." Matthew 28:18-20
- *Thy right hand, O Lord, is majestic in power,* ***Thy right hand, O Lord, shatters the enemy.*** *And in the greatness of Thine excellence Thou dost overthrow those who rise up against Thee; Thou dost send forth Thy burning anger, and it consumes them as chaff. Exodus 15:6-7*
- *It will also come to pass that* ***before they call, I will answer; and while they are still speaking, I will*** *hear. Isaiah 65:24*
- *Even from eternity I am He; and there is none who can deliver out of My hand;* ***I act and who can reverse it?*** *Isaiah 43:13*
- *Now then go, and* ***I, even I, will be with your mouth****,* ***and teach you what you are to say****. But Moses said to the people, "Do not fear! Stand* ***by and see the salvation of the Lord which He will accomplish for you today****; for the Egyptians whom you have seen today, you will never see them again forever.* ***The Lord will fight for you while you keep silent****. And you are to speak to him and put the words in his mouth; and I, even* ***I, will be with your mouth*** *and his mouth,* ***and I will teach you what you are to do****." Exodus 4:12-15*
- *That the Lord spoke to Moses, saying, "I am the Lord; speak to Pharaoh king of Egypt* ***all that I speak to you****." Exodus 6:29*
- ***You shall speak all that I command you…*** *Exodus 7:2a*
- *And so, as those who have been chosen of God, holy and beloved, put on a heart of compassion, kindness, humility, gentleness and patience; bearing with one another, and forgiving each other, whoever has a complaint against anyone; just as the Lord forgave you, so also should you.* ***And beyond all these things put on love, which is the perfect bond of unity.*** *Colossians 3:12-14*

- *For if you remain silent at this time, relief and deliverance will arise for the Jews **from another place** and you and your father's house will perish. **And who knows whether you have not attained royalty for such a time as this?** Esther 4:14*
- *Truly I say to you, whatever you shall bind on earth shall be bound in heaven; and **whatever you loose on earth shall be loosed in heaven.** Matthew 18:18*
- <u>***I will give you the keys of the kingdom of heaven***</u>*; and whatever you shall bind on earth shall be bound in heaven, and whatever you shall loose on earth shall be loosed in heaven. Matthew 16:19*
- *He who overcomes**, I will make him a pillar in the temple of My God**. Revelation 3:12a*
- ***The first-born of your sons*** *(daughters in our case)* ***you shall give to Me.*** *Exodus 22:29b*

But this wasn't the only decision to make. Once we felt God was leading us to home school, we then had hundreds of decisions to make for curriculum and associations. Here are some more journal entries during the process.

<u>Prayer Journal entry:</u>
2/13/05 Begged God to help us in the process.
2/26/05 We are looking into whether to use home satellite equipment or to rent DVDs with classes on them.
5/23/05 We purchase home satellite equipment because it is the best bargain.
6/27/05 We need help. The satellite doesn't seem to be working. We try all kinds of things all summer long to get it working, but nothing works.

8/13/05 On this day we finally realized that the satellite wasn't going to work no matter what—all the possible solutions had been examined. As a family we talked about the option of DVDs, but at this time we didn't have the $1200 needed to order them. We were all sitting in our car and I remember just starting to pray out loud about it. I said, "Lord, you know we don't have this money right now. But if you want us to use the DVDs then please have a big amount of money show up right away. Otherwise we will look in a different direction for Beth."

8/14/05 Ike gets word that our family has received a gift of $2,000 from an anonymous source. We order the DVDs with hearts full of praise.

8/26/05 The DVDs arrive.

11/22/05 Beth gets her first-quarter grades. She is doing well. The DVDs seem to work well with my ministry, which is constantly on the go. Beth has become my partner in ministry and Beth is learning responsibility through the independent process of home schooling. What seemed to be a terrible set of circumstances has turned out to be a great blessing…just like it was for Naomi.

The Lord knows the days of the blameless; and their inheritance will be forever. They will not be ashamed in the time of evil; And in the days of famine they will have abundance. Psalm 37:18-19

3

DANCING IN CONFLICT

In the third year of Cyrus king of Persia a message was revealed to Daniel, who was named Belteshazzar; and the message was true and one of great conflict, but he understood the message and had an understanding of the vision. In those days I, Daniel, had been mourning for three entire weeks. I did not eat any tasty food, nor did meat or wine enter my mouth, nor did I use any ointment at all, until the entire three weeks were completed. And on the twenty-fourth day of the first month, while I was by the bank of the great river, that is, the Tigris, I lifted my eyes and looked, and behold, there was a certain man dressed in linen, whose waist was girded with a belt of pure gold of Uphaz. His body also was like beryl, his face had the appearance of lightning, his eyes were like flaming torches, his arms and feet like the gleam of polished bronze, and the sound of his words like the sound of a tumult. Now I, Daniel, alone saw the vision, while the men who were with me did not see the vision; nevertheless, a great dread fell on them, and they ran away to hide themselves. So I was left alone and saw this great vision; yet no strength was left in me, for my natural color turned

to a deathly pallor, and I retained no strength. But I heard the sound of his words; and as soon as I heard the sound of his words, I fell into a deep sleep on my face, with my face to the ground. Then behold, a hand touched me and set me trembling on my hands and knees. And he said to me, "O Daniel, man of high esteem, understand the words that I am about to tell you and stand upright, for I have now been sent to you." And when he had spoken this word to me, I stood up trembling. Then he said to me, "Do not be afraid, Daniel, for from the first day that you set your heart on understanding this and on humbling yourself before your God, your words were heard, and I have come in response to your words. But the prince of the kingdom of Persia was withstanding me for twenty-one days; then behold, Michael, one of the chief princes, came to help me, for I had been left there with the kings of Persia. Now I have come to give you an understanding of what will happen to your people in the latter days, for the vision pertains to the days yet future." And when he had spoken to me according to these words, I turned my face toward the ground and became speechless. And behold, one who resembled a human being was touching my lips; then I opened my mouth and spoke, and said to him who was standing before me, "O my lord, as a result of the vision anguish has come upon me, and I have retained no strength. For how can such a servant of my lord talk with such as my lord? As for me, there remains just now no strength in me, nor has any breath been left in me." Then this one with human appearance touched me again and strengthened me. And he said, "O man of high esteem, do not be afraid. Peace be with you; take courage and be courageous!" Now as soon as he spoke to me, I received strength and said, "May my lord speak, for you have strengthened me." Then he said, "Do you understand why I came to you? But I shall now return to fight against the prince of Persia; so I am going forth, and behold, the prince of Greece is about to come. However, I will tell you what is inscribed in the writing of truth.

Yet there is no one who stands firmly with me against these forces except Michael your prince." Daniel 10:1-21

It's not so much what I don't understand about this passage that bothers me, but what I do understand. An approximately 85-year-old man was willing to fast and pray over his nation for three weeks. To be honest, most days I won't even skip dessert over my nation's spiritual condition. This bothers me.

It bothers me that while Daniel was willing to give up so much of his life to see spiritual revival, running away with God three times every day and, at times, for long periods of intercession, I sometimes watch the clock as I fulfill my spiritual commitments. This bothers me.

It bothers me that my prayers are still so trite and self-focused while Daniel's are so grand and full of self-denial. On a similar note, I recall that Elijah asked God to withhold rain for years and thereby risked his own survival for the sake of his nation. God answered his short-term prayer for no rain, and also his long-term prayer for spiritual revival; God gave him food and water in the midst of a drought. What an amazing thought! Daniel evidenced the same kind of sacrificial prayer. His mourning over Israel brought him great personal discomfort: exhaustion along with perplexity. Yet he prayed on for understanding. He did not pray for relief, comfort or resources. When I compare my prayer lists and note the differences it bothers me.

It bothers me to see that the main lesson of this chapter is that when we pray, God listens and immediately responds, and yet so few of us are willing to give Him the time of day. This bothers me. The fact that our intercession parts the waters of circumstance to accomplish God's purposes in our world is incredible and scary at the same time; God really listens and responds! It is scary that we so seldom take Him up on His offer.

It bothers me that Daniel isn't recorded planning "events" for his fellow Jewish brothers. He does not seem to be involved in producing worship services, in doing evangelism or even teaching discipleship. Yet he is highly esteemed by God. What's more, he doesn't ever seem "too busy to pray," even with his great responsibilities as second in command over the most powerful kingdom on earth. Somehow he has carved out time for important things like prayer and fasting, and yet has managed not only to do his job, but to do it without slothfulness or negligence. I am bothered by the fact that although my responsibilities are not as great as Daniel's, when my life's pace gets frantic I find that my effectiveness is sometimes compromised.

I have asked the Lord to use these bothersome thoughts to take me to a new level in prayer, to irritate me enough that I will turn aside and seek heavenly encounters more than earthly pleasures and accomplish eternal victories even at the cost of personal comforts.

In the third year of Cyrus king of Persia a message was revealed to Daniel, who was named Belteshazzar; and the message was <u>true and one of great conflict</u>, but he <u>understood the message</u> and had <u>an understanding of the vision</u>. Daniel 10:1

As bizarre as this dream is, it is true. We can believe it. It describes a great conflict and this conflict is one that occurs every moment of "time" as we know it. The conflict continues day and night and this is why our prayers are necessary at all times. For example, note Paul's words of encouragement:

And he said to me, "These words are faithful and true; and the Lord, the God of the spirits of the prophets, sent His angel to show to His bond-servants the things which must shortly take place." Revelation 22:6

What we don't understand in God's Word is God's department. What we do understand in God's Word is our department. Because there's plenty in this passage that I *do* understand, I'm to keep busy applying its message to my life.

In those days I, Daniel, had been mourning for three entire weeks. I did not eat any tasty food, nor did meat or wine enter my mouth, nor did I use any ointment at all, until the entire three weeks were completed. Daniel 10:2-3

Daniel teaches us a little about fasting in this passage. He had been fasting for three weeks, avoiding "tasty" food and consuming no wine. This could mean that he ate bread and water alone, having given up pleasurable food for that which simply sustains life. Remember he was approximately eighty-five to ninety years old at the time. He also chose not to use Persian "after-shave" or ointment to soothe his skin. In other words, he was moved to change his lifestyle by his compassion for his nation. The remarkable thing is, God noticed. We always want to do big things for God, but here it is the little things that get the Lord's attention: Daniel went without; Daniel went with less; Daniel showed honor for God and God responded with spiritual victory and truth. To me this is one of the most important points of this lesson. Each one of us is capable of giving God the gift of little things. When we honor those in authority over us, God sees and smiles. When we put others before ourselves, He notices and is glad. When we seek spiritual revival, when we honor Him above all others, when we humble our own proud hearts, when we choose obedience over pleasure…He is pleased.

And on the twenty-fourth day of the first month, while I was by the bank of the great river, that is, the Tigris, I lifted my eyes and looked, and behold, there was a certain man dressed in linen, whose waist was girded with {a belt of} pure gold of Uphaz. His body also was like beryl, his face had the appearance of lightning, his eyes were like flaming torches, his arms and feet like the gleam of polished bronze, and the sound of his words like the sound of a tumult. Now I, Daniel, alone saw the vision, while the men who were with me did not see the vision; nevertheless, a great dread fell on them, and they ran away to hide themselves. So I was left alone and saw this great vision; yet no strength was left in me, for my natural color turned to a deathly pallor, and I retained no strength. But I heard the sound of his words; and as soon as I heard the sound of his words, I fell into a deep sleep on my face, with my face to the ground. Daniel 10:4-9

We know where Daniel was on the twenty-fourth day of the first month. He was by the river praying. What were you doing on the twenty-fourth day of the month? For a man like Daniel to have prayed three times a day there had to be a journey of growth in prayer. If you are going to become a person who prays three times a day, you must begin by being a person who prays one time a day, then two times a day, etc. I remember when my greatest challenge was simply having a quiet time every day of each month. And I am looking forward to the time when I will be able to say that I have come to the Lord three times <u>each day</u> in a month. You don't begin with fasting for twenty-one days. You begin with fasting for one meal, then two, then more as the Spirit prompts you. Daniel had a reputation for prayer. You don't get a reputation for what you "want" to do, but for what you actually do.

Let's now consider what I believe is a more significant question. What was Daniel *not* doing on the twenty-fourth day of the first month? In other words, what activities did he sacrifice so that he could pray by the river for twenty-one days straight? For other captives in Babylon there might have been parties, pleasures, and business ventures, but not for Daniel. Daniel demonstrated that you can squeeze life into what's left after prayer or squeeze prayer into what's left after life.

Daniel chose prayer and it brought the true mark of spiritual success: esteem by God. What earthly honors can compare to this? Who cares if you are in society's <u>Who's Who</u>, but if you find yourself in God's book of <u>Who's Who</u>, that is exciting! The world's trophies will gather dust and decay, but the honor of God's esteem goes on forever. Where have you been putting your attention? Have you been aiming at becoming the top salesperson, being parent of the year, getting a high degree of education or being the one who dies with the most toys? Some of these things have their place, but they are nothing compared to being noticed and approved of by the Most High God. What was it that got God's attention? Was it Daniel's knack for perfection? No, it was his spiritual hunger and the recognition of his spiritual poverty. These are qualities that we are all capable of experiencing.

Daniel began his life in Babylon as a young man with high principles and honor for the Lord. We've seen his encounters as a middle-aged man making faithful commitments and influencing world leaders by his example. And now we see the blessings of a righteous man of old age. He is involved in heavenly conflicts. According to James, the effective prayers of a righteous man avail much. Our first challenge in the Christian life is to conquer self, choosing discipline and obedience over selfishness and pleasure. Our next challenge is to work on our witness to others by overcoming fear with faith, anger with patience, hatred with compassion. But in the latter years of an effective Christian's life, the battle can move into heavenly arenas where we press back spiritual forces. There is an additional benefit to consistent prayer: by hanging around God's workshop of prayer, sooner or later you'll probably get a chance to see some of the projects He's working on. This was the case for Daniel when he encountered the heavenly visitor who was sent to give him an important message. Who was the heavenly messenger that Daniel met? Some say it was an epiphany, a pre-incarnate visitation of Jesus Christ. It might have been. There are some definite similarities to other descriptions of the Holy One, as in the Book of Revelation.

And in the middle of the lampstands one like a son of man, clothed in a robe reaching to the feet, and girded across His breast with a golden girdle. And His head and His hair were white like white wool, like snow; and His eyes were like a flame of fire; and His feet were like burnished bronze, when it has been caused to glow in a furnace, and His voice was like the sound of many waters. And in His right hand He held seven stars; and out of His mouth came a sharp two-edged sword; and His face was like the sun shining in its strength. And when I saw Him, I fell at His feet as a dead man. And He laid His right hand upon me, saying, "Do not be afraid; I am the first and the last, and the living One; and I was dead, and behold, I am alive forevermore, and I have the keys of death and of Hades. Revelation 1:13-18

And to the angel of the church in Thyatira write: The Son of God, who has eyes like a flame of fire, and His feet are like burnished bronze, says this. Revelation 2:18

I, however, agree with <u>A Commentary Critical, Experimental and Practical of the Old and New Testaments</u> (by the Rev. Robert Jamieson, D.D., Rev. A. R. Fausset, A.M. and the Rev. David Brown, D.D. Wm. B. Eerdman's Publishing Co., Grand Rapids, MI, p. 441) that it might have also been an angel in his truest, majestic form. Awesome? Yes! Frightening? Yes! I don't see any indications in the text to convince me that the being who appears in verse four is not the same one who appears in verse ten. The change in his appearance may provide an important clue.

Here is the description given for the visitor: a linen garment, a belt of pure gold, his body like beryl, his face like lightning, eyes like flaming torches, arms and legs like polished bronze, and a voice like a tumult.

And behold, a severe earthquake had occurred, for an angel of the Lord descended from heaven and came and rolled away the stone and sat upon it. And his appearance was like lightning, and his garment as white as snow; and the guards shook for fear of him, and became like dead men. And the angel answered and said to the women, "Do not be afraid; for I know that you are looking for Jesus who has been crucified." Matthew 28:2-5

And the seven angels who had the seven plagues came out of the temple, clothed in linen, clean and bright, and girded around their breasts with golden girdles. Revelation 15:6

And I saw another strong angel coming down out of heaven, clothed with a cloud; and the rainbow was upon his head, and his face was like the sun, and his feet like pillars of fire. Revelation 10:1

We have to be careful not to tamper with the text. There are three sections that deal with a heavenly visitor. One of them is verses 4-9; another is verses 10-15. The last section is verse 16 through the revelation of the vision in chapter 11. We know that in sections two and three it is definitely an angel, and most likely Gabriel. Other than Daniel's response we don't have any indication that in section one it is not the same angel. What puzzles us is that the visitor in section one and the one spoken of in section three seem different in appearance. I personally believe that all three sections speak of the same angel. To me this explains why everyone who ever sees an angel has the reaction of fear. Why else would each one begin with, "Fear not!"? At the same time we are told to care for strangers because we might entertain angels "unaware." Hebrews tells us plainly that it is possible to be feeding an angel when indeed you think you are feeding a human being. I believe that these sections are meant to teach us some things about angels: what they can and cannot do, and how they appear. There are things we can do that angels can't. There are things angels can do that we cannot. Let us each do the things that we can to win the battle.

Then behold, a hand touched me and set me trembling on my hands and knees. And he said to me, "<u>O Daniel, man of high esteem</u>, understand the words that I am about to tell you and stand upright, for I have now been sent to you." And when he had spoken this word to me, I stood up trembling. Then he said to me, "Do not be afraid, Daniel<u>, for from the first day that you set your heart on understanding {this} and on humbling yourself before your God, your words were heard, and I have come in response to your words.</u> But the prince of the kingdom of Persia was withstanding me for twenty-one days; then behold, Michael, one of the chief princes, came to help me, for I had been left there with the kings of Persia. Now I have come to give you an understanding of what will happen to your people in the latter days, for the vision pertains to the days yet {future.}" And when he had spoken to me according to these words, I turned my face toward the ground and became speechless. Daniel 10:10-15

God notices something as simple as an attitude. Good or bad, God sees every intention of the heart. That's why we are told to pay attention to the desires of our hearts also. From the very moment Daniel begins to seek understanding and humbles himself, God responds. What does this mean for us? What do you need to understand? Begin asking the Lord today to send help your way.

Where have you tried your own way and failed? Humble yourself at this very moment so that God might send His strength and direction your way. Psalm 139:4 says that the Lord knows my words before they are even on my tongue.

This passage teaches us even more about angels. They are given designated areas of authority. Michael is over Israel. We see that in verses 21 and in 12:1 Gabriel seems to have been assigned to Darius. A high-ranking demon seems to be in charge of Persia. Just as there are angels and archangels, there seems to also be a hierarchy in the demon world.

This heavenly conflict is interesting since it takes place during the time period that the first group of Jews returned to Israel. A heavenly conflict is taking place over "the nations" on a daily basis. Centers of power on earth are connected to warring forces in the heavenlies.

For our struggle is not against flesh and blood, but against the rulers, against the powers, against the world forces of this darkness, against the spiritual forces of wickedness in the heavenly places. Ephesians 6:12

Daniel teaches us that our prayers make the difference in the outcome of the battle. Your daily prayers are affecting world forces. Does this help you get out of bed and on your knees? What commissioned messenger will get through today because of your prayers?

A friend of mine recently sent me an interesting web link. It appeared to be a beautiful rose and we were encouraged to click our mouse over its petals. When we did this, it appeared that the flower was underneath water and the click produced ripples just as if we had touched its watery covering. In like manner the nations respond to our prayers. We pray and ripples of action are sent out by heavenly response. Expand your prayers to nations today.

Affect ruling powers and territories with your faith pressings. See the Kingdom of God expanded and the enemy's strongholds removed.

And another angel came and stood at the altar, holding a golden censer; and much incense was given to him, that he might add it to the prayers of all the saints upon the golden altar which was before the throne. And the smoke of the incense, with the prayers of the saints, went up before God out of the angel's hand. And the angel took the censer; and he filled it with the fire of the altar and threw it to the earth; and there followed peals of thunder and sounds and flashes of lightning and an earthquake. Revelation 8:3-5

First of all, then, I urge that entreaties and prayers, petitions and thanksgivings, be made on behalf of all men, for kings and all who are in authority, in order that we may lead a tranquil and quiet life in all godliness and dignity. This is good and acceptable in the sight of God our Savior, who desires all men to be saved and to come to the knowledge of the truth. 1 Timothy 2:1-4

With all prayer and petition pray at all times in the Spirit, and with this in view, be on the alert with all perseverance and petition for all the saints, and pray on my behalf, that utterance may be given to me in the opening of my mouth, to make known with boldness the mystery of the gospel. Ephesians 6:18-19

Elijah was a man with a nature like ours, and he prayed earnestly that it might not rain; and it did not rain on the earth for three years and six months. And he prayed again, and the sky poured rain, and the earth produced its fruit. James 5:17-18

Does our president have an assigned angel? Do our prayers really affect national decisions and movements? YES. Daniel was a one man prayer army. His prayer requests were answered in the morning newspaper. So if our nation is going to pot you can blame your own dismal prayer life. You can make a difference. You can shake demonic authorities right out of their comfort zones. You can influence world powers from your living room. The fight is real. Paul says that Satan thwarted his plans in I Thessalonians 2:18. What are Satan and his workers trying to thwart in your family? What are his designs on your city? What is his plot toward your nation? Fight back today with some time spent in prayer by the river, or by the bed, or at your desk.

For the weapons of our warfare are not of the flesh, but divinely powerful for the destruction of fortresses. We are destroying speculations and every lofty thing raised up against the knowledge of God, and we are taking every thought captive to the obedience of Christ. 2 Corinthians 10:4-5

And behold, one who resembled a human being was touching my lips; then I opened my mouth and spoke, and said to him who was standing before me, "O my lord, as a result of the vision anguish has come upon me, and I have retained <u>no strength</u>. For how can such a servant of my lord talk with such as my lord? As for me, there remains just now <u>no strength</u> in me, nor has any breath been left in me." Then {this} one with human appearance <u>touched me again and strengthened me.</u> And he said, "O man of high esteem, do not be afraid. Peace be with you; take courage and be courageous!" Now as soon as he spoke to me, <u>I received strength</u> and said, "May my lord speak, for <u>you have strengthened me</u>." Then he said, "Do you understand why I came to you? But I shall now return to fight against the prince of Persia; so I am going forth, and behold, the prince of Greece is about to come. However,

I will tell you what is inscribed in the writing of truth. Yet there is no one who stands firmly with me against these {forces} except Michael your prince." Daniel 10:16-21

The vision left Daniel physically weak. His fasting also left him weak. Yet an angel gave him strength. He "felt" different, vibrant and strong, after a spiritual encounter with a mere angel. The implications of this are important, for they show us that it is the inner man who can strengthen the outer man. It is not the other way around. Physical pleasures will never encourage our spiritual-man. But seeking the higher things, the better things, can strengthen us and help us accomplish amazing things.

Therefore we do not lose heart, but though our outer man is decaying, yet our inner man is being renewed day by day. 2 Corinthians 4:16

Elijah also experienced the strengthening of an angel. See 1 Kings 19:4-8. The angel touched him and gave him food. Elijah then lay down and slept. Then the angel touched him again and gave him more food.

Now may our Lord Jesus Christ Himself and God our Father, who has loved us and given us eternal comfort and good hope by grace, comfort and strengthen your hearts in every good work and word. 2 Thessalonians 2:16 -17

But the Lord is faithful, and He will strengthen and protect you from the evil one. 2 Thessalonians 3:3

But the Lord stood with me, and strengthened me, in order that through me the proclamation might be fully accomplished, and that all the Gentiles might hear; and I was delivered out of the lion's mouth. 2 Timothy 4:17

That He would grant you, according to the riches of His glory, to be strengthened with power through His Spirit in the inner man. Ephesians 3:16

The devil likes to insinuate to us that "going forward" with God will mean trouble. He wants us to think, if only in the most subconscious realm, that intercession will drain us and that the cost of spiritual warfare will be too high for us to pay. When he slithers up beside you to plant seeds of fearful theology, it is critical to remember that Daniel's weakness was met with strength, that Elijah's hunger was met with food and that the children of Israel lacked nothing in the wilderness. Prove that Satan's plantings have no place in your garden by turning aside for some extra prayer time today. While you're at it, ask that his highest-ranking workers might be rendered immobile and that angelic messengers would be sent out to strengthen the saints all over the world. Ha!

Prayer Journal entry:
8/16/05 In a very brief way, I describe to our countywide prayer group that I believe the Lord has been encouraging me to begin an Intercessor's Network. I tell them that I want to know who prays where and when in Riverside County and that I would like to have some means of communicating with them the needs that affect all of us in our county.
8/31/05 I am invited to meet Pastor Raul Diaz of *Path of Life Church* in Riverside, California. His small church of about one hundred people has been working with the City of Riverside to help care for the homeless. My friend Libby Collier of *Turn Ministries* is trying to get prayer support for him. She feels that the Lord's timing for beginning the Intercessor's Network is NOW.

His church has been operating a homeless shelter at March Air Force Base and has offered to run it permanently, but the city says it is closing all its shelters and that *Path of Life* doesn't have enough money to operate it. In passing we also learn that Pastor Diaz needs sanitary kits to give to people. I mention it to our children's director, Stephanie.

The next Thursday I am invited to meet with the pastors of Riverside to initiate the Intercessor's Network, which will help us know about needs that affect the bigger picture of our county. We intercede for Pastor Raul and the shelter issue. We have a wonderful time of worship and unity.

In November of 2005 we get word that the city has already opened one shelter under the operation of *Path of Life*, that they are continuing to encourage them to raise funds for the March Air Force Base shelter, and that they will possibly open an additional shelter under their supervision. Wow! Possibly three shelters operated by contract between the County of Riverside and a church!

On the first Sunday of December, (2005) my friend Libby will come to our church and received an abundant supply of survival kits that have been assembled by our children in Sunday school. Praise the Lord!

Prayer Journal entry:
2/28/05 I hear that our bus needs $4500 of work and that the church doesn't have it right now.
6/26/05 The bus locks up just before the end of second service and cannot be moved. We take those who ride the bus home in several cars.
6/27/05 I am praying intensely over the bus. It is such a lifeline for those who ride it. As I am praying, a tow truck arrives to take the bus. Miraculously the bus "unlocks" and doesn't need the supposed repairs. Thank you Lord!

4

DANCING ON THE WATER

If you are going to be in connection with Jesus, the living God, there will be times when you end up, if even momentarily, *waltzing* on the water. I am speaking figuratively here, not literally. Peter was a man, just like us, but one night the Lord intended for him to experience the steps of a lifetime when he actually *walked on the water*! Yes, obedience to Jesus will take us through the fire, through trouble and even through the valley of the shadow of death. But if we are honest, we must also agree that waltzing with Jesus ends up taking us through incredible blessing and fantastic miracles. Many times we place our attention on the fact that Peter looked at the waves around him and sank into the water. But think for a moment about the faith that put Peter on the water and let him experience what no other human being has ever done; he *actually walked on the water*! What a tremendous blessing he experienced. Can you imagine him re-telling the story to his children and grandchildren? When we walk with God, blessings must be expected. Even unrealistic expectations can become realistic prayer requests, because God is God. We are told in Psalm 23:5 of *The*

Living Bible: *"You provide delicious food for me in the presence of my enemies. You have welcomed me as your guest, blessings overflow!"* *The Message* indicates that this blessing from the Lord is like a six-course meal. (Not only does David expect God to give him victory over his enemy, but he compares the blessings of God to his enjoying a bountiful banquet with his enemy looking on.)

    I experienced just such a time in 2005. I had begun praying about my desire for a harp. Nine years previously I had sold my harp to pay some of our bills. Now our church was doing a musical that had a harp part, and so I had sheepishly entered the prayer request in my notebook. I felt, in a way, that I didn't have a leg to stand on in asking such an impractical thing. It wasn't a necessary thing like food or shelter. It was just a whim, a desire. I did remind the Lord about Matthew 19:29, which says: *"And everyone who has left houses or brothers or sisters or father or mother or children or fields for my sake will receive a hundred times as much and will inherit eternal life."* *(NIV)* "I don't want a hundred harps," I jested with the Lord, "just one." (See also Mark 10:29 and Luke 18:29.) I also noted the promise of Psalm 21:2: *"You have given him his heart's desire, and You have not withheld the request of his lips. Selah."* *(NASB95)* and Psalm 84:11b-12 *"No good thing does He withhold from those who walk uprightly. O LORD of hosts, how blessed is the man who trusts in You!"* *(NASB95)*

    It wasn't long after that day that I was searching for harps on the Internet and happened to stumble across a website with a harp testimony (http//home.swbell.net/schref/story.html). Martha Schreffler told of seeing a vision during her prayer time of her playing a harp which was being used for a healing ministry. This seemed strange at the time because she didn't even own a harp! She had played one many years before, but didn't have the finances for such a thought. You'll have to read the entire story, but one year later, she indeed had a harp, completely paid for, and was using it in a healing ministry. Wow! I remember reading that and thinking, "God, are you trying to get me to believe you for a harp?" I remember responding that day with a heart of faith.

Not long after, I began sending out some inquiring e-mails. I needed three things: a used harp (new ones cost way too much), a small harp (I was looking for one I could transport in my car trunk—although that didn't happen), and I was looking for a company that would work creatively with the financing. In less than six weeks I had located a new harp company near my home that had ONE used harp, a small 40-string pedal harp, and they were willing to do what I needed to finance the project. The day our friend Dale brought the harp from the store to my house (remember, it didn't end up fitting in my trunk), I was so overwhelmed. God had answered this prayer that seemed too big and had done it effortlessly. It made me wonder, "What other things is God is just waiting to do for me that I can't believe Him enough to even ask about?" What are your deepest dreams and desires? Have you asked the Lord to fulfill them?

God doesn't always take our breath away by such quick answers to our prayers, but if what you are asking is what He wants to do, and if this is the time He wants to do it, bam! You have it! God's will and His timing are so critical. Even one day can be too late for Him. The children of Israel wandered for thirty-eight years, and then out of the blue, God said, "Today" is the day to go up into the Promised Land.

Now the time that it took for us to come from Kadesh-Barnea until we crossed over the brook Zered, was thirty-eight years, until all the generation of the men of war perished from within the camp as the Lord had sworn to them. Deuteronomy 2:14

You shall cross over Ar, the border of Moab TODAY. Deuteronomy. 2:18

Perhaps you have been praying long over someone's salvation, or a job, or a marriage, or… Consider this: Today may be just the day God wants to see victory. Today may be the end of the trial and the wandering. I wonder if any of the Israelites prayed daily over the second chance to go up into the land. I can almost bet that Caleb did. He knew what was ahead. He had seen the grapes. He had seen the conquering work of God. He wanted his inheritance to be more than a mirage. Can you imagine his response when Moses announced, "Today the Lord said we should go up." I can almost picture him dancing through the camp, an eighty-five year old man with fire in his eyes, hurrying the others to get into position and scolding those who seemed to dawdle.

It is dangerous to try to do something when it's not God's timing. It is equally dangerous not to do something He has asked you to do when it is His timing. (See Numbers 14:40-45 and 13:30.) This is the best thought: How dangerous, how life-changing, how impacting the prayer can be that is lined up with God's perfect will and timing. Today could be that day! Pray prayers that actualize promises TODAY. Pray prayers that occupy and possess your inheritance TODAY.

Prayer Journal entry:
4/14 I asked the Lord for a pedal harp.
5/20 I asked again for a harp.
5/12 I felt pricked to believe for a harp after reading a woman's testimony on the internet. She felt God tell her that she would have a harp ministry in a time of intercession. Yet, she did not have a harp and no means of getting one.
5/30 I found out a new Salvi harp store had opened in Anaheim. (All other stores were quite a distance away from my house.)
5/31 Purchased harp and our friend Dale said he would pick it up for me tomorrow.

6/1 I have a harp!
6/3 I got an anonymous gift of $100 for my "harp fund."
6/9 I found out who gave that $100 – surely this was faith at work. The gift came from a friend who had been out of work for several months. God had prompted her to give it. I believe God honored her tremendous gift and her faith.

 Sometimes when you have been in the ministry for awhile, you can fall into the habit of a ministry *moaning* mentality. "I can't afford to do that...my husband is a pastor." "We live in this neighborhood, not that one." Do you get the picture? I was reading about the Israelites not too long ago, and my attitude seems like theirs at times. In their case, God had provided water and food for millions of Jewish people. He had kept their clothes from wearing out and protected them from the diseases of the Egyptians. Yet they were never satisfied. Their moaning and whining made God sick. Last week on a plane trip, I caught myself responding with similar comments to the two people seated next to me, when I heard the Lord speak to my heart, "Didn't I give you a harp? Haven't I paid all your bills? Didn't I give you new carpet and new tile throughout your house?" (The story of the carpet is in my second book, <u>Warring at the Window</u>. The Lord also sent a gift of new tile last year.) Didn't I give you two sets of living room furniture? I could feel myself sinking lower in the seat. Right there I realized what a BAD billboard I am sometimes for the Lord's care. He is such a good God. He has cared for our family through so much and provided again and again, and I can't even give Him the credit He deserves.
 If you and I are going to really "waltz" with Him, we will both need to learn to celebrate the privilege of being His people, of dwelling in the midst of His presence (like the Israelites) and having Him care for our every need as we take the journey through life's wilderness. There are times we will just experience water

from rock and dinner from the sky if we are going to be led by the *Living* God. We will need to learn that a small crowd and a big God are all that's needed to win a crucial battle. And when He has performed mighty and miraculous things that go beyond what we could even dream or imagine, we must learn to praise Him, not just in our hearts or in the congregation, but on the streets to the ones who haven't known such care.

For the Lord your God has blessed you in all that you have done; He has known your wanderings through this great wilderness. These forty years the Lord your God has been with you; <u>you have not lacked a thing</u>. Deuteronomy 2:7

<u>But for all this, you did not trust the Lord your God</u>, who goes before you on your way to seek out a place for you to encamp, in fire by night and cloud by day, to show you the way in which you should go. Deuteronomy 1:32-33

  There's something funny about waltzing with the Lord. Whatever you could believe Him for today is never good enough for what He wants you to believe Him for tomorrow. If you have learned to trust Him for lunch, then He moves you one more step to trust him for the rent. When you can trust Him for that, there is a new challenge right around the bend.
  When we started adding employees to our church I began to pray fervently for their paychecks. It seemed a big responsibility back in 1999 to pray over four church employees (three were part time) and seven school employees. Today I pray over fifteen church employees and thirty-two school employees. From eleven to forty-seven represents much growth. That kind of responsibility can be overwhelming. Fear is our greatest foe. The reason God has given us many years of different kinds of trials has been to grow

our trust and belief in His ability. The Lord gives us on-the-job training to help us succeed as we grow.

Be strong and brave. Don't be afraid of them and don't be frightened, because the Lord your God will go with you. He will not leave you or forget you. Deuteronomy 31:5-6 (NCV)

Every God-begotten person conquers the world's ways. The conquering power that brings the world to its knees is our faith. The person who wins out over the world's ways is simply the one who believes Jesus is the Son of God. 1 John 5:4-5 (MSG)

Just like Peter, in the middle of our walk with God, the walls may seem too high for us and we may be tempted to move out of step with Him in order to save ourselves or our ministry from what looks like impending disaster. It is at times like these that we must put on the mentality of Caleb and Joshua. It is not our job to evaluate the high city walls. It is not our job to estimate the manpower needed to take out the giants. It is not for us to contemplate our own grasshopper feebleness when possessing what God has promised. It is our job to believe God!

I remember a conversation once where someone was explaining why a particular group hadn't moved "forward" in their area of ministry. "Do you know what obstacles we were facing?" I was asked. I remember my response, and I believe it even today, "I don't care what the obstacles are. The obstacles aren't our problem." There is nothing the enemy can throw at us that can defeat us if we believe. That is why giving attention to our faith is the most important thing we can do. We must nurture it. We must surround ourselves with Calebs and Joshuas, lest we find ourselves turning back at crucial times where faith is our only effective weapon. The only limits that we put on God are the things for which we cannot believe Him.

*In addition to all, taking up the shield of faith with which you will be able to extinguish **all** the flaming missiles of the evil one. Ephesians 6:16*

One way to strengthen our faith is to record and remember all the things that He has done. That is why I love my prayer journal. I always record the date of each prayer request and when it was answered. I always like to color the request in with a highlighter after the Lord has answered it. Now, after many years of consistent praying, I browse page after page of colored-in, fulfilled prayers. This is such a testimony of God's faithfulness!

Year after year you can see the entries on my list for Vacation Bible School. There are usually many requests for leadership, resources and help. We just finished our fifteenth Vacation Bible School as a church and, as usual, God met every need. He really gave us a special "diamond" year gift: We did Group Publishing's *Jerusalem Marketplace* experience. We had the extra challenge of wanting everyone in a Bible time costume. (That was over four hundred costumes worth of faith.) He was up to the challenge, as usual. He provided costumes, scenery, artisans for our marketplace, food, water, staff, children and, most important, many salvations. You would think that after fifteen years of faithfulness, we wouldn't ever have trouble trusting the Lord. But if we spend too much time looking at the resources needed and not enough time looking at the Resource Giver we get off track. It's so easy to get off track. And there are constantly new people in our "camp" who haven't experienced the last fifteen years of faithfulness and they must be taught to trust.

Just make sure you stay alert. Keep close watch over yourselves. Don't forget anything of what you've seen. Don't let your heart wander off. Stay vigilant as long as you live. Teach what you've seen and heard to your children and grandchildren. Deuteronomy 4:9 (MSG)

It's not good enough to just make it through your wilderness. The Lord wants us to be intentional about remembering all the ways He has helped us. Over and over He tells Israel that they have forgotten what He has brought them through (Ezekiel 16:22, 43) and what He as done for them (Ezekiel 16:10-14). We find God admitting it makes Him angry. How do you intentionally remember what God has done? He goes on to say that in addition to simply remembering what He has done, we are to pass it on to the next generation. Do you intentionally share with your children and grandchildren when the Lord answers your prayers? How do they know when God has helped you in a time of need? How would we have known that Peter walked on the water if someone hadn't written it down (as inspired by the Holy Spirit) for future generations to read?

When you are full, don't forget to be reverent to him and to serve him and to use his name alone to endorse your promises. Deuteronomy 6:13 (TLB)

And know this day that I am not speaking with your sons who have not known and who have not seen the discipline of the Lord your God-- His greatness, His mighty hand, and His outstretched arm ...but your own eyes have seen all the great work of the Lord which He did. Deuteronomy 11:2-7

Surely, if we are in connection with the all-powerful God, we will dance a dance at times that defies the limitations of this world. We will remove mountains, we will watch demons flee and we will see the multitudes fed with a boy's lunch. When we dream dreams that allow us to see up Heaven's ladder, let us intentionally set up markers, as Jacob did, to show others yet to come that God is real and that He hears the prayers of His people. Let us be the scribes who record spiritual battles where God's Spirit leads us to victory. Let us be the letter writers who chronicle God's care in shipwrecks and storms. Then others who pass by the same way will read our accounts and gain new strength for their missionary journeys.

One area in which I experienced God's faithfulness was through the provision of a Christian education. I had enrolled at Azusa Pacific College. (Now it is a university.) I was getting ready to leave for school when my father pulled me aside and asked, "How do you expect to pay for all this?" I remember responding that I believed with all my heart that God wanted me at this very institution and that He would provide what was needed. I had exactly $500 saved towards my expenses. Smile. Four years later I graduated with no loans and all bills paid. This was a modern-day miracle. (If you are a student at a Christian university today, you may need your faith to be strengthened by reading this account.) After one year of teaching I went back to seminary. I began at Western Evangelical Seminary (outside Portland, Oregon). By this time, at the ripe old age of 22, I had matured enough to know there was no logical way I could pay for all the expenses of school with a part-time job waiting tables at a family steak house so I made the Lord a deal. I told the Lord that I would give Him a 33% tithe if He would help take care of all my expenses. (I don't generally recommend making "deals" with God, and keeping my end of this one was particularly challenging, but the Lord took me up on it.) A year later I had to leave seminary because of some health issues. I had a hyperactive thyroid and no insurance, but I left debt-free. Praise the Lord! The Lord then provided free medical care at the City of Hope ($15,000 worth of surgery), future seminary classes at Azusa's Graduate School of Theology and a steady supply of resources that paid for all the expenses related to my schooling.

The Lord doesn't always work in the same way. I can't guarantee that He will take you through your schooling with no loans or that He will provide you with a beautiful harp, but of one thing I am sure, no one who plants their trust in the Lord will be disappointed. He is no respecter of persons. He hears the prayers of obedient sons and daughters all the time. He fulfills their deepest desires *easily*.

Just the other day I was talking to a young man about trusting the Lord to care for him in ministry. I had to tell him how the Lord had cared for me by providing schooling and medical care and the amazing experience of not even needing to take out a loan to do it. All around us are those who are just putting on their dancing shoes. We must be careful to pass on the records of dancing on the ceiling so they will know what to dream about and ask for in their prayers. Watching our lives are future Arthur Murrays, who will be teaching *the dance* to others. Let us leave footsteps they can follow.

Prayer Journal entry:
5/18/05 Felt the Lord was leading me to do a ministry event for pastors' wives. I do not have any budget or personal funds for this endeavor. I begin praying.
6/13/05 I ask our local radio station to do announcements for this event. Their current rules say they can't because the event is not "for everyone."
During the preparation for the event, the Lord ministers to my heart through Matthew chapter seventeen. He shows me that in order to move mountains you must have prayer and fasting. I obey. He encourages me to enlist a prayer warrior for each table of pastors' wives. I ask Him to move two mountains: to get the pastors' wives to come and to get our radio station to change their mind and make the announcements. Reservations up to this point

have been few. I have had many ladies from my church volunteer to decorate a table. I would like guests for each of their tables.

7/21/05 The radio station decides to make an exception and make our announcements.

7/31/05 Forty pastors' wives are ministered to at our event: *Return to the Nest for Some Rest*. The tables are decorated with bird's nests, the food is plentiful for our ninety guests and much ministry takes place through the speaker Cyndi, the worship Matt and the intercessors. Another church in town (Calvary Chapel Corona) donates money to purchase decorations and food, and the people of the Olive Branch go way beyond the call of duty to provide more food and door prizes for the pastor's wives. My friend Cindy of Women's Fitness Retreat donates a free year-long gym membership to each pastors' wife, and my friend Priscilla of Liberty Tax Service gives each one a coupon for a free tax preparation. The day is a delightful waltz on the water for all of us!

5

DANCING IN THE FIRE

Shadrach, Meshach and Abed-nego faced an opportunity to dance in the fire with the Lord. They had no idea HOW He would answer their prayers, but their feet never faltered as they followed Him with trustful steps. How can we grow to be like them? They were confident people in the face of a crisis. Why is our confidence often so segregated from the desired outcome of our praying? Let's take a look at this passage to discover its truths.

Nebuchadnezzar the king made an image of gold, the height of which was sixty cubits and its width six cubits; he set it up on the plain of Dura in the province of Babylon. Daniel 3:1

We are told that one cubit is about eighteen inches. This means that the idol constructed was nine by ninety feet. It was impressive. It was a towering influence over Babylonian culture.

Then Nebuchadnezzar the king sent word to assemble the satraps, the prefects and the governors, the counselors, the treasurers, the judges, the magistrates and all the rulers of the provinces to come to the dedication of the image that Nebuchadnezzar the king had set up. Daniel 3:2

  Everybody who was anybody was invited. All of the positions listed are a symbol of the world's authority and power and they are all going to bow <u>to somebody</u>. Satan wants it to be himself but the one true God demands worship alone.
  Israel's biggest problem had been that of wandering out of God-worship and into putting other things on golden pedestals. It's our problem too; we keep getting our passions out of order. For example, what is your number one passion? Is it your family, your job or your dreams? Nebuchadnezzar is not the only one constructing idols that assume the place of honor that belongs to God alone. Whether our constructions are temporary or permanent, they must be torn down as soon as they are identified.
  Anything to which you bow is your master, even if it is just mental bowing. It reminds me of the little boy being punished by having to sit in the corner. He says, "I might be sitting down on the outside, but I'm standing up on the inside." You might be showing honor to the Lord on the *outside*, but *inside* you might believe that your problems are too big for Him to handle. 2 Corinthians 10:5 talks about strongholds set up against the knowledge of God. Let's do some demolishing today of phony imposter-gods that have taken up residence in our own minds.

The giant step in the walk of faith is the one we take when we decide God is no longer a part of our lives. He is our life. Beth Moore

Then the satraps, the prefects and the governors, the counselors, the treasurers, the judges, the magistrates and all the rulers of the provinces <u>were assembled</u> for the <u>dedication of the image</u> that

Nebuchadnezzar the king had set up; and they stood before the image that Nebuchadnezzar had set up. Daniel 3:3

Who was the image being dedicated to? The god Bel was worshipped throughout Babylonia. So in actuality, they were assembled to honor demons. Thank goodness these three godly young men understood that diversity in who we worship is not worship at all. How I wish it was as clear for the young people of our generation!

What do I mean then? That a thing sacrificed to idols is anything, or that an idol is anything? No, but I say that the things which the Gentiles sacrifice, they sacrifice to demons, and not to God; and I do not want you to become sharers in demons. You cannot drink the cup of the Lord and the cup of demons; you cannot partake of the table of the Lord and the table of demons. What do I mean then? That a thing sacrificed to idols is anything, or that an idol is anything? No, but I say that the things which the Gentiles sacrifice, they sacrifice to demons, and not to God; and I do not want you to become sharers in demons. 1 Corinthians 10:19-21

While Israel remained at Shittim, the people began to play the harlot with the daughters of Moab. For they invited the people to the sacrifices of their gods, and the people ate and bowed down to their gods. So Israel joined themselves to Baal of Peor, and the Lord was angry against Israel. Numbers 25:1-3

Then the herald loudly proclaimed: "To you the command is given, O peoples, nations and men of every language, that at the moment you hear the sound of the horn, flute, lyre, trigon, psaltery, bagpipe, and all kinds of music, you are to fall down and worship the golden image that Nebuchadnezzar the king has set up. But whoever does not fall down and worship shall immediately be cast into the midst of a furnace of blazing fire." Daniel 3:4-6

The people are given a command from the king. They were required not only to obey, but to do it immediately. We can take a lesson from all those who worshipped the image. They obeyed and they did it immediately. If the people of Christianity were assembled and what God had commanded us to do was known, would the world see us obeying and doing it immediately?

Therefore at that time, when all the peoples heard the sound of the horn, flute, lyre, trigon, psaltery, bagpipe, and all kinds of music, all the peoples, nations and men of every language fell down and worshiped the golden image that Nebuchadnezzar the king had set up. Daniel 3:7

All the people did what they were told to do. Everyone was watching for dissenters. These three did not do what everybody else did. We don't pay that much attention to those who go along with the crowd, but dissenters stand out like a sore thumb. The fact that Chick-fil-A is not open on Sunday gets your attention more than all the businesses that are. Is your life one that is attracting attention or are you blending in with everyone else?

For this reason at that time certain Chaldeans came forward and brought charges against the Jews. They responded and said to Nebuchadnezzar the king: "O king, live forever! You yourself, O king, have made a decree that every man who hears the sound of the horn, flute, lyre, trigon, psaltery, and bagpipe, and all kinds of music, is to fall down and worship the golden image. But whoever does not fall down and worship shall be cast into the midst of a furnace of blazing fire. There are certain Jews whom you have appointed over the administration of the province of Babylon, namely Shadrach, Meshach and Abed-nego. These men, O king, have disregarded you; they do not serve your gods or worship the golden image which you have set up." Daniel 3:8-12

The Chaldeans are jealous of the position of the Jewish young men in their government. Even though Daniel saved their lives eighteen years before this incident by interpreting the king's dream, their gratitude has vaporized with the memory. We too can be jealous with others around. We can learn from the Chaldeans how *not* to handle that jealousy. Don't say things to try to hurt others. Don't worry about "positioning" yourself for promotion. Live honorably and you will be noticed. Even if the world doesn't honor you, the Lord will.

Then Nebuchadnezzar in rage and anger gave orders to bring Shadrach, Meshach and Abed-nego; then these men were brought before the king. Nebuchadnezzar responded and said to them, "Is it true, Shadrach, Meshach and Abed-nego, that you do not serve my gods or worship the golden image that I have set up? Now if you are ready, at the moment you hear the sound of the horn, flute, lyre, trigon, psaltery, and bagpipe, and all kinds of music, to fall down and worship the image that I have made, very well. But if you will not worship, you will immediately be cast into the midst of a furnace of blazing fire; and what god is there who can deliver you out of my hands?" Shadrach, Meshach and Abed-nego answered and said to the king, "O Nebuchadnezzar, we do not need to give you an answer concerning this matter. If it be so, our God whom we serve <u>is able to deliver us</u> from the furnace of blazing fire; and <u>He will deliver us</u> out of your hand, O king. <u>But even if He does not</u>, let it be known to you, O king, that we are not going to serve your gods or worship the golden image that you have set up." Daniel 3:13-18

Three statements that the young men make in this passage hook our hearts: He is able to deliver us, He will deliver us and even if He does not… All three statements represent levels of faith. Where are you on this growth scale? Are you learning what God can do? (He can provide my house payment this month.) Are you able to believe Him for what He will do? (He will provide my house payment this month.) Or are you trusting Him even when He is not doing what you think needs to be done? (I trust Him even if, for some reason, He does not provide my house payment this month.) John Wesley points out in his commentary that these three "were resolved to suffer rather than sin." Their faith is not that of young Christians, even though they are young men.

Though He slay me, I will hope in Him. Job 13:15

Let no one look down on your youthfulness, but rather in speech, conduct, love, faith and purity, show yourself an example of those who believe. 1 Timothby 4:12

Then Nebuchadnezzar was filled with wrath, and his facial expression was altered toward Shadrach, Meshach and Abed-nego. He answered by giving orders to heat the furnace seven times more than it was usually heated. And he commanded certain valiant warriors who were in his army to tie up Shadrach, Meshach and Abed-nego, in order to cast them into the furnace of blazing fire. Daniel 3:19-20

Some valiant men died that day for no good reason. Men who had gone out and fought battles valiantly died in avoidable *circumstances*. What a waste! But at the same time, our three heroes became valiant warriors, willing to die for a great cause: the honor of the King of Heaven. Many valiant warriors in God's kingdom die doing ordinary things. Today your life can be given teaching the next generation in preparation for the end times or you can live life and die for no particularly good reason or cause. You can take up space on this earth and die, without offering this world the slightest benefit.

Then these men were tied up in their trousers, their coats, their caps and their other clothes, and were cast into the midst of the furnace of blazing fire. For this reason, because the king's command was urgent and the furnace had been made extremely hot, the flame of the fire slew those men who carried up Shadrach, Meshach and Abed-nego. But these three men, Shadrach, Meshach and Abed-nego, fell into the midst of the furnace of blazing fire still tied up. Then Nebuchadnezzar the king was astounded and stood up in haste; he responded and said to his high officials, "Was it not three men we cast <u>bound</u> into the midst of the fire?" They answered and said to the king, "Certainly, O king." He answered and said, "Look! I see four men loosed and walking about in the midst of the fire without harm, and the appearance of the fourth is like a son of the gods!" Daniel 3:21-25

Three times we are told that these men were thrown in tied up: verse twenty-one, twenty-three (still tied up) and twenty-four, (bound). Great detail is given so that we might be convinced of the encumbrance of their attire and shackles. Yet the emphasis in verse twenty-five is that they were loosed and walking around. The crackling fire that we so desire to avoid is the very place where we lose our shackles. The fire is where we learn about God's authority. The fire is where we experience God Almighty. This is why we can dance in the midst of the flames while holding His hand. If these three had never entered the fiery place, they would not have known that the Lord could meet them within it. And so it is with the trials you and I experience. They show us who God is in the midst of the difficulty and pain.

Four months before my mother died, she married Rev. Don Spicer. It was a whirlwind courtship, but the Lord brought these two together for a mighty purpose. (Sometimes the Lord works in a way that we would consider slow, but sometimes His quick work takes our breath away.). He used the joy of their love to help my mother through the pain of her cancer and He gave us a new grandpa for comfort in the absence of both sets of our parents. As we have come to know Poppa Don better, we have seen the quality of his life and ministry, and we are proud to have him in our family tree. Poppa Don's first wife was stricken with Alzheimer's and he spent eight years caring for a wife who could not speak, feed herself or walk unassisted. What a difficult road the Lord required of Don. And yet, when he speaks of it, he gives testimony to the fact that the Lord helped him. The Lord got him through and with honor. If you are never in the fire, you don't understand that the Lord can be in there with you.

And the angel of the Lord appeared to him in a blazing fire from the midst of a bush; and he looked, and behold, the bush was burning with fire, yet the bush was not consumed. So Moses said, "I must turn aside now, and see this marvelous sight, why the bush is not burned up." When the Lord saw that he turned aside to look, God called to him from the midst of the bush, and said, "Moses, Moses!" And he said, "Here I am." Then He said, "Do not come near here; remove your sandals from your feet, for the place on which you are standing is holy ground." He said also, "I am the God of your father, the God of Abraham, the God of Isaac, and the God of Jacob." Then Moses hid his face, for he was afraid to look at God. Exodus 3:2-6

As I studied this related passage, I was struck by God's position in the fire. From where is God calling? He's in the midst of the fire. He's IN THE FIRE ITSELF. Don't get off track with the "sights" of God. It's not enough to be near the burning bush. God called to Moses from the midst of the burning bush. So *in* the fire is a good place to be. It's where God introduces Himself to us.

The "sight" of the flame first caught Moses' attention, but the experience of meeting the God of the fire got his lifetime commitment. Do you want to be satisfied looking at the fire that didn't burn men up, or do you want to get in it and hear what Jesus is saying? You can spend your life walking around the furnace and looking in, but if you want to get near to the heart of Jesus you'll have to release the fear of "being burned."

One of my fears is big dogs. I come face to face with this fear every Wednesday when we go door to door sharing Christ with people in the neighborhood surrounding our church. Because of my fear, we always pray over "the dogs" before we head out. One day we had parked our car, shared up and down the block and then gotten back into our car when out of nowhere came one huge pit bull and his little side-kick companion. They were barking something in dog language that surely meant, "Get out of here right now or we'll rip you to shreds." I was trying to comply by driving my car down this dirt road but the dogs kept following, trying to bite my tires. The fact that I was in a big, moving car didn't seem to bother them a bit.

Another time I had walked up a long driveway and was just about to hang a brochure on the front door when I suddenly noticed a very quiet and composed Doberman looking straight into my eyes. A quick glance surmised that his chain was long enough to allow him to reach the front door comfortably and I immediately decided NOT to evangelize that house that day. Smile. However, each week I am joined by a young-at-heart friend named Louise. She understands the power of God which makes her frame more powerful than mine, even though she is my senior. She takes authority over all dogs that we encounter in the name of Jesus. As much as I hate these dog encounters, I am learning from Louise that God is in these situations with us. I am learning that He has authority over Dobermans and pit bulls, and though my faith is not on the level of Shadrach, Meshach and Abed-nego, perhaps some day it will be as a result of friends like Louse and others. I assure you that whatever your big dog, you will face it at some point or another because God wants to show you that He's bigger than big dogs (big waves, big bills, big problems and, of course, hot fires). Why are you trying to avoid the very experiences that will accomplish all this? The fire is nothing to fear. Being without God is something to fear.

And do not fear those who kill the body, but are unable to kill the soul; but rather fear Him who is able to destroy both soul and body in hell. Matthew 10:28

Then Nebuchadnezzar came near to the door of the furnace of blazing fire; he responded and said, "Shadrach, Meshach and Abed-nego, come out, you servants of the Most High God, and come here!" Then Shadrach, Meshach and Abed-nego came out of the midst of the fire. <u>*And the satraps, the prefects, the governors and the king's high officials gathered around*</u> *and saw in regard to these men that the fire had no effect on the bodies of these men nor was the hair of their head singed, nor were their trousers damaged, nor had the smell of fire even come upon them. Daniel 3:26-27*

      All the witnesses that God appointed for that day realized there had been no effect on their bodies. Their clothes had not been singed or damaged, there was no smell of smoke on them, but the ropes were gone. The same fire that burns your bonds won't singe your clothing. This is the power of our God. <u>God wanted all the satraps, prefects, governors and high officials to SEE IT</u>. That's why He had them all assembled that day. His perfect plan was getting them all to worship Him, even though they didn't even go to church. When you come across some terrible "pickle" this week and you feel you are forced to take a stand in the midst of the crowd at work or school or in your neighborhood, just realize that God is taking church outside the walls. He is using your life to get the world's attention and show them who the real God is.

Nebuchadnezzar responded and said, "Blessed be the God of Shadrach, Meshach and Abed-nego, who has sent His angel and delivered His servants <u>who put their trust in Him</u>, violating the king's command, and <u>yielded up their bodies</u> so as not to serve or worship any god except their own God. Therefore, I make a decree that any people, nation or tongue that speaks anything offensive against the God of Shadrach, Meshach and Abed-nego shall be torn limb from limb and their houses reduced to a rubbish heap, inasmuch as there is no other god who is able to deliver in this way." Then the king caused Shadrach, Meshach and Abed-nego to prosper in the province of Babylon. Daniel 3:28-30

     Do you trust Him enough to yield up your body? The kind of devotion God requires is like the difference between the chicken and the pig helping to provide breakfast. For one, it's a mere contribution. For the other, it's complete sacrifice. God is looking for people who are completely offered up as a living sacrifice for Him.
     Today when you refuse to bow to the world's ideas and end up in hot circumstances, do a tango of faith with the Lord in the midst of the heat.

<u>Why does God allow fiery furnaces?</u>
- To bless us. God never tests us without a plan for blessing, i.e., Abraham with a son, Job with a double portion,

Shadrach, Meschach and Abed-nego with His divine presence, Daniel with authority and honor. So take heart if you feel you are being tested. There's good news up ahead.
- As a witness to those who aren't saved and an example to those who are saved. It shows others how to act in these circumstances. To see someone care for a dying spouse, a rebellious teenager, or someone with a hardened heart is training for future challenges we may face. Circumstances are teachers. It's easier to learn from others' trials.
- To burn off our bonds – the only thing burned off was the ropes/bonds. The fire of God can burn off your limitations without burning YOU. The refiner's fire reveals our bondages, our addictions and our wounds. Fiery furnaces change *us*, not necessarily our circumstances.
- To show off God's fantastic power.

<u>With what kind of friends are you hanging around?</u>
Who you hang around with determines how you will act in the decisions you make when you face your fiery furnaces.
- Those that understand who God is. There are no mental boxes (limitations) allowed where the Living God of the universe is concerned.
- Those who live by <u>His</u> law, and this overrides the "law of the land" at times.
  o Midwives in Egypt – God allowed the law so they could honor Him above it. He in turn blessed them and gave them households of their own. *But the midwives feared God, and did not do as the king of Egypt had commanded them, but let the boys live. Exodus 1:17 So God was good to the midwives, and the people multiplied, and became very mighty. Exodus 1:20 And it came about because the*

> *midwives feared God, that He established households for them. Exodus 1:21*
- Moses as he left Egypt. *By faith he left Egypt, not fearing the wrath of the king; for he endured, as seeing Him who is unseen. Hebrews 11:27*
- Peter and John with respect to evangelism.
- Those who aided Jews under the Nazi regime.
- Those who aided those caught in slavery in America.
- Those who are committed to seeing the terrible crime of abortion stopped in America.

You are not bound by any law that contradicts the laws of God. <u>We must be found on the right side of God's law, even though it puts us on the wrong side of man's law.</u>

<u>The fire is there so our faith can put it out.</u>

We are told in the following Scripture verses that God allows some pretty terrible circumstances for another reason: so our faith can eliminate them. Yes, sometimes the fiery furnace or the fiery dart is there so that our faith can extinguish it.

Who by faith conquered kingdoms, performed acts of righteousness, obtained promises, shut the mouths of lions, <u>quenched the power of fire,</u> escaped the edge of the sword, from weakness were made strong, became mighty in war, put foreign armies to flight. Hebrews 11:33

In addition to all, taking up the shield of faith with which you will be able to <u>extinguish all the flaming missiles</u> of the evil one. Ephesians 6:16

Sometimes God allows the furnace to take us through *the fire* to *glory.*
  Not too many martyrs write books about their experiences. They can't tell us what it was like to die a death by torture, but I believe God has a special grace for these kinds of circumstances. Otherwise, how could Stephen be seen looking into Heaven with a glow on his face while he was being stoned? Unless some people face fiery furnaces that actually burn, we would not be able to see the saving fire of God IN the fire.

It is a special privilege to be chosen for persecution.
And I saw thrones, and they sat upon them, and judgment was given to them. And I saw the souls of those who had been beheaded because of the testimony of Jesus and because of the word of God, and those who had not worshiped the beast or his image, and had not received the mark upon their forehead and upon their hand; and they came to life and reigned with Christ for a thousand years. Revelation 20:4

  So if you are standing in or near a fiery furnace today, take heart. God can save you. He will save you. And even if His method is not the one you were hoping for, He will use this testing to further the progress of the gospel, to bless you, and to bring praise and glory to Himself.

Paul from prison: *Now I want you to know, brethren, that my circumstances have turned out for the greater progress of the gospel.* Philippians 1:12

And others were tortured, not accepting their release, in order that they might obtain a better resurrection; and others experienced mockings and scourgings, yes, also chains and imprisonment. They were stoned, they were sawn in two, they were tempted, they were put to death with the sword; they went about in sheepskins, in goatskins, being destitute, afflicted, ill-treated (men of whom the world was not worthy), wandering in deserts and mountains and caves and holes in the ground. Hebrews 11:35b-38

Prayer Journal entry:
Found out that the County of Riverside wants to charge our church a $125,000 re-development fee. They want to charge for the building we are already using plus the new building that is nearing completion. This fee would need to be paid before the building could ever be used. We go to prayer.
10/19/05 The fee is lowered to $3,000. Praise the Lord!

Prayer Journal entry:
One day my seat belt broke. The car dealer wants an exorbitant amount of money to fix it. I know we can't afford that much. I go into prayer and remind the Lord that it's a law to wear a seat belt. While praying, a little idea pops into my head. As I get back into my car, I realize that my shoulder strap can go all the way into the middle seat belt clasp. I drive this way for quite awhile.
5/10/05 Ike is able to purchase a replacement part and to fix my seat belt.

Prayer Journal entry:
9/22/05 My trunk latch broke one Wednesday after Bible study. The dealer wants $800 to fix it. I ask the Lord for His help. We don't have that kind of money right now. The dealer gets it to shut temporarily but warns me not to open it up. My Bible study materials are in the trunk and I need them. I open the trunk and try to shut it; it clicks shut. The trunk isn't all the way shut so I can't get a car wash, but at least it stays shut without having to be wired.
10/05/05 Ike has time to work on the car and he gets it fixed permanently for FREE.

Prayer Journal entry:
We have invited a Korean choir to visit our church. They have been with us before and the Lord has really used them to minister. We pick them up at 10 p.m. on a Saturday night. We are planning on feeding them breakfast, having them minister at our services, and then we have been told that their next church will be feeding them lunch. After I bring the pastor and the bus driver to our home, the pastor informs me that WE are supposed to feed all twenty-eight of them tomorrow for lunch. I have a standing rule that I honor the Sabbath, so I will not go to the store on Sunday. I make a decision to trust the Lord to help me feed them. I find one roast and a chicken in my freezer. I will take a couple of cake mixes to church and bake them in between services.

The Lord provides help from Connie, Cal, and Marti. Jim goes home and picks his orange tree for us. Kathy brings rice, pie and ice. All twenty-eight people have plenty to eat and we have witnessed the Lord work another miracle.

6

DANCING IN BESIEGEMENT

Have you ever felt that you were being personally attacked by Satan? Have you ever experienced a period of time where you, your family and your obedience seem to be in the crosshairs of the enemy's sights and that the forces of evil had been united to crush you and your zeal for the Lord? I have been called on to intercede for some who have felt just this way. I have also gone through times of besiegement in my own ministry. We are not alone. There have been others who have felt this same way throughout the centuries. *(Therefore, since we have so great a cloud of witnesses surrounding us... Hebrews 12:1)* Job could relate and his life lays out lessons to encourage us. In addition, 1 Kings 20 is a fascinating passage full of strategy for just such times. It is stacked with lessons and so we will deal with them verse by verse.

*Now Ben-hadad king of Aram gathered **all his army**, and there were **thirty-two kings** with him, **and horses and chariots**. And he went up and **besieged Samaria, and fought against it.** Then he* *sent messengers to the city to Ahab king of Israel, and said to him, "Thus says Ben-hadad,* ***'Your silver and your gold are mine; your most beautiful wives and children are also mine.*** *'" 1 Kings 20:1-3*

Notice how the odds *seem* to be stacked in this situation. Here is tiny Israel against an alliance of thirty-two powers. The enemy is only pointing out the obvious: there are more of us than there are of you. You <u>will be</u> defeated. And I <u>will be</u> the authority over everything of value that you have. His first course is getting you to believe that you are ***outnumbered*** and ***under resourced.***

Whether you are praying for your nation or your family, the enemy wants you to feel defeated before you ever begin. He knows that your prayers WILL accomplish great things. He knows that the best defense is to stop you before you ever get started, so naturally, he targets your thought processes. He wants you to feel overwhelmed and inadequate in this endeavor. Why pray over world-wide events, when you have no control over them? Why labor over your church's decisions if you are not one who makes them? Why prayer-walk your city when you don't have any means to influence its leaders? There are so many needs. How could you pray over them all? What difference could prayer make anyway? We need a newness of mind to begin our offensive attach each day.

You are from God, little children, and have overcome them; because greater is He who is in you than he who is in the world. 1 John 4:4

But you will chase your enemies, and they will fall before you by the sword; five of you will chase a hundred, and a hundred of you will chase ten thousand, and your enemies will fall before you by the sword. Leviticus 26:7-8

Is anything too difficult for the Lord? At the appointed time I will return to you, at this time next year, and Sarah shall have a son. Genesis 18:14

Ah Lord God! Behold, Thou hast made the heavens and the earth by Thy great power and by Thine outstretched arm! Nothing is too difficult for Thee. Jeremiah 32:17

During times of besiegement we must focus our thoughts and worship on God. He created the entire world and everything in it in just six days. He holds not only OUR universe—as big as that is to conceive with our limited scope and vision—but the expanses of the heavens are also in His hands. He removes kings from power. He tells the ocean where to stop on the sand. Not only can He do all that, but He also responds to the tiniest cry for help. We drop the pebble of prayer into His pond and He responds with ripple upon ripple of action. Your ability to remember and be diligent over prayer requests might be feeble, but His ability to care for each one you lift to Him is infinite. His responses to our inadequate requests are perfectly just and ordered. So focus on Him and you will see how the resource tables are turned in each and every situation.

Every prayer requires response from the Lord. For the forgiven, it is impossible to pray impotent prayers. Therefore pray with confidence. The Lord has no trouble hearing your requests, the Holy Spirit has no problem editing them to line up with God's perfect will (Romans 8), and He has absolutely no boundaries on His abilities, so pray away. Pray unabashedly. Pray prayers that make His mouth open in amazement and mountains move in response because God is God. Moving mountains is what He can do easily. Don't let overwhelming circumstances become your thirty-two kings, making you immobile and convincing you to give up.

*And the king of Israel answered and said, "**It is according to your word, my lord**, O king; **I am yours, and all that I have**." 1 Kings 20:4*

Whether it is through the media or your mind, the next battle field of the enemy is convincing you that *his word* is the authority. Words are important to the enemy because they direct hearts and actions. He spends much time over the minds of those who write textbooks and print newspapers, because he wants us to **believe what he says through them**. We have to be careful, though, because our enemy is the father of lies and we know that if his lips are moving, he's got to be tampering with truth. Is this statement the king makes true? Are we HIS (the enemy's)? No. We have been bought with a price. Therefore, we need to reject any claims to ownership or lordship that the enemy makes over our lives and resources.

For you have been bought with a price: therefore glorify God in your body. 1Corinthians 6:20

You were bought with a price; do not become slaves of men. 1 Corinthians 7:23

But you are a chosen race, a royal priesthood, a holy nation, a people for God's own possession, that you may proclaim the excellencies of Him who has called you out of darkness into His marvelous light. 1 Peter 2:9

And because you are sons, God has sent forth the Spirit of His Son into our hearts, crying, "Abba! Father!" Galatians 4:6

Now follow me through the mental steps of being a purchased "love servant" of Jesus Christ. The Lord can certainly take us through any trial if He wants to. We are HIS. Everything we possess is HIS also, but that is the only way anything can touch us...THROUGH HIM (our master and Lord). The enemy cannot put his hands on anything that belongs to God without going THROUGH HIM. Now here is a new thought the Lord gave recently: if all that belongs to us belongs to our master and Lord, why do we have trouble claiming the lives of family members? If my toaster belongs to God because He is my Lord, why not my rebellious child and my ungodly city also? Everything that is mine is His. *(It is also true that everything that is His is mine, but that would lead us to another lesson and away from our text.)* As you pray, remind God that it is *your* neighborhood, *your* city, *your* household, *your* nation and that it has all been given over to His ownership as your Lord and master. So in essence, as a result of the transference of ownership, it is His child's future for which you are interceding. It is His city for which you are pleading revival. It is His people, His nation that needs radical spiritual intervention. *(Not to mention His claim to ownership as a result of creation!)*

Moses understood this concept. He pleaded for the Lord's presence to go with them while God was still angry with Israel because of their rebellion with the golden calf.

Now therefore, I pray Thee, if I have found favor in Thy sight, let me know Thy ways, that I may know Thee, so that I may find favor in Thy sight. Consider too, that this nation is Thy people. *Exodus 33:13*

For how then can it be known that I have found favor in Thy sight, I and Thy people? *Is it not by Thy going with us, so that we, I and* Thy people, *may be distinguished from all the other people who are upon the face of the earth? Exodus 33:16*

Let's get back to our text. Ahab is king over Israel at this time. What do we know about him? We know that He was the most wicked ruler who ever held Israel's throne. He certainly does not have any personal reasons to expect God's intervention in the situation other than the fact that these are "God's people" and "His treasured possessions."

Now Ahab the son of Omri became king over Israel in the thirty-eighth year of Asa king of Judah, and Ahab the son of Omri **reigned over Israel in Samaria twenty-two years**. *And Ahab the son of* **Omri did evil in the sight of the Lord more than all who were before him**. *1 Kings 16:29-30*

Later on, in time, we will see a radical life change in Ahab as a result of a prophetic message where God gives Ahab this ultimatum: *And Ahab said to Elijah, "Have you found me, O my enemy?" And he answered, "I have found you, because you have sold yourself to do evil in the sight of the Lord. Behold, I will bring evil upon you, and will utterly sweep you away, and will cut off from Ahab every male, both bond and free in Israel; and I will make your house like the house of Jeroboam the son of Nebat, and like the house of Baasha the son of Ahijah, because of the provocation with which you have provoked Me to anger, and because you have made Israel sin. And of Jezebel also has the Lord spoken, saying, 'The dogs shall eat Jezebel in the district of Jezreel.' The one belonging to Ahab, who dies in the city, the dogs shall eat, and the one who dies in the field the birds of heaven shall eat." Surely there was no one like Ahab who sold himself to do evil in the sight of the Lord, because Jezebel his wife incited him. And he acted very abominably in following idols, according to all that the Amorites had done, whom the Lord cast out before the sons of Israel.* **And it came about when Ahab heard these words, that he**

tore his clothes and put on sackcloth and fasted, and he lay in sackcloth and went about despondently. *Then the word of the Lord came to Elijah the Tishbite, saying,* ***"Do you see how Ahab has humbled himself before Me?*** *Because he has humbled himself before Me, I will not bring the evil in his days, but I will bring the evil upon his house in his son's days."* ***And three years passed without war between Aram and Israel.*** *1 Kings 21:20-22:1*

This incident we are studying today falls **after** Elijah tells Ahab and Jezebel that there will be no rain. (What seems to us to be a time of spiritual *drought* turns out in actuality to be a season for underground spiritual *watering* which eventually produces a national revival.) It is **after** the mighty contest on Mount Carmel where the forces of light and darkness are clearly identified by all of Israel and a nation unites to follow the true God. It is **after** Elijah's encounter with the awesome display of God's power and the intimate message of a still small voice. It is just prior to Ahab wanting and getting Naboth's vineyard (via murder). It is before he honestly comes humbly before the Lord and repents. All of that is just to show that Ahab was not in a great spiritual condition at this time. He has built Asherahs (idols) throughout the land. His wife is an evil woman who will kill a man for a garden. But because he is the king over God's people and because God loves him and wants to display His mighty saving power in his life, God evens the odds that are stacked against him. Whether you are in a position of authority or not, God loves YOU and wants to display His mighty power in YOUR life. The enemy will try to point out your weaknesses and failures. You might hear him ask, "Why should God want to answer YOUR prayers in a time of besiegement?" Remember this: God even heard Ahab's prayers! He is looking for a humble, repentant heart. That is all He needs to move in the circumstances that are besieging your life and provide victory.

Ahab isn't a spiritual man, living by the Word of God, so he listens to the voice of the enemy. There are lots of people who day after day choose to listen to the speeches of the enemy. They tune into his wavelengths and are fed by his daily broadcasts. They refuse daily supplements of the Word of God and are left to the brainwashing of the enemy. Don't listen to his propaganda! If you do, the day may come when you, like Ahab, may start turning over the control of your life dreams. His propaganda can pulverize your prayers if you believe it.

Then the messengers returned and said, "Thus says Ben-hadad, 'Surely, I sent to you saying, "You shall give me your silver and your gold and your wives and your children," but about this time tomorrow I will send my servants to you, and they will search your house and the houses of your servants; and it shall come about, whatever is desirable in your eyes, they will take in their hand and carry away.'" 1 Kings 20:5-6

The enemy is not happy with just ownership. He wants possession. The mindset that all you have and are belongs to him is not enough. He wants to direct you in a slave-like fashion. He wants to see you bend the knee to his plans and desires. He is not happy with anything but immediate obedience.

He aims his attacks at what you care about most. This passage hits the nail on the head: "Whatever is desirable in your eyes." Give up each treasure into the hands of Jesus early on. Relinquish your rulership over them to Christ as the Lord of your life. You will find that His methods for safe-keeping are impenetrable and secure.

Then the king of Israel called all the elders of the land and said, "Please observe and see how this man is looking for trouble; for he sent to me for my wives and my children and my silver and my gold, and I did not refuse him." And all the elders and all the people said to him, "Do not listen or consent." 1Kings 20:7-8

Such a powerful truth is found here: do not listen or consent. First we must remove our ears from hearing all that the enemy desires to do, and second, we must not give permission to his ideas, either mentally or physically. This is not always an easy thing to do. He slithers up while we are thinking about tasty fruit and plants the seeds of his theology in conversations we never authorized. We must quickly leave his presence and his impromptu marketing session or we will find ourselves hiding out later with a freshly opened gift of "sin-sickness." Where have you paused in his presence lately? What slugs of truth has he tried to pass for the Real McCoy in your thinking? Do not listen or consent!

The enemy reminds me of a door-to-door salesman. I don't always know in advance what he is promoting, but I know this, that if I stand there listening to his pitch long enough, I'll probably end up buying something I don't need or want. He is convincing me to desire something I don't have and he is very good at what he does. So don't even open the door!

So he said to the messengers of Ben-hadad, "Tell my lord the king, 'All that you sent for to your servant at the first I will do, <u>but this thing I cannot do</u>.'" And the messengers departed and brought him word again. And Ben-hadad sent to him and said, "May the gods do so to me and more also, if the dust of Samaria shall suffice for handfuls for all the people who follow me." 1 Kings 20:9-10

The enemy threatens and boasts, but you start winning the battle when you begin to call his bluff. You are not *his*. Your family, your treasures and your dreams do not belong in his arena of authority. Once you begin to acknowledge these things you will see that he no longer has the power to influence and control your life. <u>The besiegement ends the day you understand his limitations and your freedoms.</u>

Then the king of Israel answered and said, "Tell him, 'Let not him who girds on his armor boast like him who takes it off.'" 1 Kings 20:11

In other words, don't boast about your victory until the war is over. Our enemy indeed puts on his armor to go to war. But the victory has already been determined by Jesus' death and resurrection and the time for him to take off his armor and walk around as the victor will never come.

There is also a message for *us* in this proverb. If we are not spiritually prepared for battle with the enemy, we shouldn't parade around like we are. Prayer and time in the Word are the means by which our armor is fitted for the day. Start the battle by protecting you and yours with the essentials of battle.

It doesn't matter how long you have been committed to prayer; there are always new challenges to face and distractions to overcome. Sometimes we get a little comfortable walking around in armor that we have worn in victory after victory. Sometimes like old soldiers we like putting on the armor and strutting around. Sometimes, that is, when our prayer posture has trouble fitting into the image we wish we were. I run into people all the time that used to be more devoted to prayer. They committed time to prayer, and God responded by using them marvelously. Maybe you used to devote much time to prayer, but lately you have been preoccupied with lesser things. Don't make the mistake of dressing up in old armor to fight new battles. God wants to make us a <u>new</u> threshing tool, fit for the new situations we face each day.

Behold, I have made you a new, sharp threshing sledge with double edges; you will thresh the mountains, and pulverize them, and will make the hills like chaff. Isaiah 41:15

And it came about when Ben-hadad heard this message, as he was drinking with the kings in the temporary shelters, that he said to his servants, "Station yourselves." So they stationed themselves against the city. 1 Kings 20:12

Just as the enemy stations himself against us, we must station ourselves against his evil plans. The stance changes from defense to offense when we begin to pray.

You need not fight in this battle; station yourselves, stand and see the salvation of the Lord on your behalf, O Judah and Jerusalem. Do not fear or be dismayed; tomorrow go out to face them, for the Lord is with you. 2 Chronicles 20:17

I will stand on my guard post and station myself on the rampart; and I will keep watch to see what He will speak to me, and how I may reply when I am reproved. Habakkuk 2:1

We see in many places throughout Scripture that the enemy sets a course of action against the people of God. He does not want to see their temple rebuilt. He is not happy about having the wall rebuilt around Jerusalem. He is not happy with the effective witness of the honorable life of Job and other heroes of the faith. When the enemy gets upset, he begins a plan. We can also see throughout Scripture that when God's people obey and persevere in spiritual temptation, the victory is *always* won. So we don't concentrate our time and attention on HIS PLANS. We place our attention on OUR OBEDIENCE.

Now behold, a prophet approached Ahab king of Israel and said, "Thus says the Lord, 'Have you seen all this great multitude? Behold, I will deliver them into your hand today, and you shall know that I am the Lord.'" 1 Kings 20:13

What a message from the Lord Ahab receives on this day! Though the enemy is a multitude, God is *guaranteeing* victory. He will deliver the enemy into Ahab's hand. But Ahab isn't the only one to whom this message is given. You are a lucky recipient also. The Lord absolutely guarantees that your enemy is defeated and you can experience it in your circumstances today. King Ahab couldn't see a tiny handful of Israelites win against a MULTITUDE and not understand the power of the true and living God. The Lord knows that as you see the enemy and his resources pressed back in your life, you will understand it also.

And Ahab said, "By whom?" So he said, "Thus says the Lord, 'By the young men of the rulers of the provinces.'" Then he said, "Who shall begin the battle?" And he answered, "You." 1 Kings 20:14

There is always a strategy to the Lord's victories. Each one is unique to its circumstances. In this case it is the young men who will lead the initial charge. They happen to be the sons of the elders who told King Ahab, "Do not listen or consent." They were spiritually in tune and their sons would lead the battle to victory. If you are out of touch with the Lord, your "listening" may be hampered by Satan's "white noise." A clear conscience and a clean life will help us to hear the voice of God. You don't have to be a prophet to experience it.

The most important question in this verse is this: who begins the battle? YOU do. When you decide that you are tired of besiegement, tired of the enemy's orders and his requests for your resources, then you can fire the first shot. You may not be a king, but you have total authority over the kingdom of your life. Are you ready for the marching orders from God that will save you and the lives of your family?

Then he <u>mustered</u> the young men of the rulers of the provinces, and there were 232; and after them he mustered all the people, even all the sons of Israel, 7,000. 1 Kings 20:15

So 7,232 went out against a *multitude* and won. Yes, one put a thousand to flight!

One of your men puts to flight a thousand, for the Lord your God is He who fights for you, just as He promised you.   Joshua 23:10

And they went out at noon, while Ben-hadad was drinking himself drunk in the temporary shelters with the thirty-two kings who helped him. And the young men of the rulers of the provinces went out first; and Ben-hadad sent out and they told him, saying, "Men have come out from Samaria." Then he said, "If they have come out for peace, take them alive; or if they have come out for war, take them alive." So these went out from the city, the young men of the rulers of the provinces, and the army which followed them. And they killed each his man; and the Arameans fled, and Israel pursued them, and Ben-hadad king of Aram escaped on a horse with horsemen. And the king of Israel went out and struck the horses and chariots, and killed the Arameans with a great slaughter. 1 Kings 20:16-21

We see several items to note in this passage. First, we see the act of obedience. The young men lead the charge, just as the Lord directed them. There is no way to victory faster than obedience. It may not seem easy and it may not always make sense, but it always leads to triumph when we trust God's wisdom over our own. Some of the things we read in God's Word don't always seem logical: lend without expecting to be repaid, cast your bread upon the waters, turn the other cheek. Yet, when God says them, He puts His own infinite understanding behind them. So if we simply do as He says, in the end victory will come. (Even if the circumstances in between don't seem so rosy.)

The second truth we see here is that they killed *each his man*. Corporate victory depends on the obedience of each individual. If each of us simply kills the flesh and seeks after God's heart, the battle is won. I can't kill *your man* and you can't kill *mine*. We each must kill our own "natural man."

Then the prophet came near to the king of Israel, and said to him, "Go, strengthen yourself and observe and see what you have to do; for at the turn of the year the king of Aram will come up against you." 1 Kings 20:22

God is so gracious and faithful. He lets the King of Israel see the future through the prophet. The King of Aram *will* come again. So He sends a message to "prepare and strengthen yourself." We don't have to have a prophet deliver this message to us. Scripture constantly warns us to be on the alert because our enemy is a roaring lion, seeking someone to devour. Our job is to prepare: to be saturated in God's Word so we can rightly divide truth and to be fortified with prayer. We know that our enemy will come to tempt us. We know that the Word of God is our sure defense, yet we sometimes view reading and studying it as optional.

Now the servants of the king of Aram said to him, "Their gods are gods of the mountains, therefore they were stronger than we; but rather let us fight against them in the plain, and surely we shall be stronger than they." 1 Kings 20:23

The enemy's first mistake is to limit God. It can also be our downfall. We may not have seen God conquer in this or that circumstance. But the limitations we put on Him become the very ones we find on us.

"And do this thing: remove the kings, each from his place, and put captains in their place, and muster an army like the army that you have lost, horse for horse, and chariot for chariot. Then we will fight against them in the plain, and surely we shall be stronger than they." And he listened to their voice and did so. So it came about at the turn of the year, that Ben-hadad mustered the Arameans and went up to Aphek to fight against Israel. And the sons of Israel were mustered and were provisioned and went to meet them; and the sons of Israel camped before them like two little flocks of goats, but the Arameans filled the country. 1 Kings 20:24-27

There are two elements of Israel's victory which can be seen long before the battle begins: they are mustered and provisioned and they are armed and resourced. Here is where, again and again, God's people fail. They dash out into each day's circumstances without prayer, without the Word of God tucked in their hearts, only to find themselves dashed into circumstances that are overwhelming to them.

Then a man of God came near and spoke to the king of Israel and said, "Thus says the Lord, 'Because the Arameans have said, "The Lord is a god of the mountains, but He is not a god of the valleys;" therefore I will give all this great multitude into your hand, and you shall know that I am the Lord.'" So they camped one over against the other seven days. And it came about that on the seventh day, the battle was joined, and the sons of Israel killed of the Arameans 100,000 foot soldiers in one day. 1 Kings 20:28- 29

God's timing is critical to the victory. We may be on the first or the fifth day of our spiritual battle and not see progress. But when God's day comes, the enemy will be defeated. So what day are you on in your trial today?

Do you remember Dr. Tony Campolo's famous message, "It's Friday, but Sunday's a Comin'?" The message originated with an elderly black preacher who began his message by painting a picture of the darkness and despair of the death of Jesus Christ. In the middle of the hopelessness, his message took a shift in tone. Yes, the disciples were confused and hurt. "But," he reminded the audience, "Sunday's a comin'." The enemy is constantly trying to get us to look at the darkness, the hopelessness that surrounds us too. But remember, no matter what day it is today, Resurrection Day is up ahead.

But the rest fled to Aphek into the city, and the wall fell on 27,000 men who were left. And Ben-hadad fled and came into the city into an inner chamber. And his servants said to him, "Behold now, we have heard that the kings of the house of Israel are merciful kings, please let us put sackcloth on our loins and ropes on our heads, and go out to the king of Israel; perhaps he will save your life." So they girded sackcloth on their loins and put ropes on their heads, and came to the king of Israel and said, "Your servant Ben-hadad says, 'Please let me live.'" And he said, "Is he still alive? He is my brother." Now the men took this as an omen, and quickly catching his word said, "Your brother Ben-hadad." Then he said, "Go, bring him." Then Ben-hadad came out to him, and he took him up into the chariot. 1 Kings 20:30-33

Not listening or consenting was the King's best move in this chapter. His worst move is inviting the enemy to ride in the seat next to him. The enemy will come and tempt, but you sure don't have to give him a box seat. Here it is, plain and simple: don't make friends with the enemy! Don't hang out with him and certainly don't make alliances with him or the things he represents.

Many times when it appears the enemy has been defeated, he simply utilizes a new strategy. He tries to become an ally. After the Lord helps Israel to win the battle of Ai, the "enemy" acts craftily and makes an unauthorized "alliance" with Israel. Had God's people sought His guidance the covenant would never have been ratified. So be aware that if you continue to be obedient during a time of spiritual besiegement, the enemy may try to get you into some partnership or alignment that will bring dishonor and a dissipation of spiritual resource. Be on the look out for it. Be wary of travelers bearing gifts and sad stories. Check each potential team member out in the presence of your righteous judge. Look both ways, physically and spiritually, before crossing intersections of decision.

Therefore do not be partakers with them; for you were formerly darkness, but now you are light in the Lord; walk as children of light (for the fruit of the light consists in all goodness and righteousness and truth), trying to learn what is pleasing to the Lord. And do not participate in the unfruitful deeds of darkness, but instead even expose them. Ephesians 5:7-11

And Ben-hadad said to him, "The cities which my father took from your father I will restore, and you shall make streets for yourself in Damascus, as my father made in Samaria." Ahab said, "And I will let you go with this covenant." So he made a covenant with him and let him go. 1 Kings 20:34

Why would we make a covenant with the enemy? Why would we make such a foolish move? It can only happen to a Christian when there is no conversation with the God of the universe. We cannot accept the promises of the enemy until we have rejected the care of our Lord.

We who are reading the chapter see the audacity of the situation. Here is the same guy who for two battles has tried to destroy Israel. Now he is making promises to restore it. The enemy has a basket of empty promises to hand you whenever you are convinced that God's care isn't sufficient for your life.

Now a certain man of the sons of the prophets said to another by the word of the Lord, "Please strike me." But the man refused to strike him. Then he said to him, "Because you have not listened to the voice of the Lord, behold, as soon as you have departed from me, a lion will kill you." And as soon as he had departed from him a lion found him, and killed him. Then he found another man and said, "Please strike me." And the man struck him, wounding him. So the prophet departed and waited for the king by the way, and disguised himself with a bandage over his eyes. 1 Kings 20:35-38

This passage is crammed with complexities and lessons. We witness one prophet who will simply not listen to the Lord. It is not enough NOT to listen to the enemy. We must make a concerted effort to LISTEN to the Lord. We must not only HEAR His voice but we must OBEY it. The Lord demands obedience from His prophets AND servants (us). Who are we to reject His instructions? The second prophet had learned that when God says to do something, He understands the "WHY" and that is all that matters. He follows through and does something that we cannot understand. He strikes a prophet. It seems to be such a ludicrous command. "Why?" we wonder. But God knows He needs a prophet with a black eye that day for an important rebuke. He must have an obedient prophet at this crucial moment. Sometimes the things God tells me to do seem ridiculous too. But I want so much to be the obedient responder on whom He knows He can count.

The only way I can understand the "why" of this passage is to see the big picture, which is rarely my perspective.

And as the king passed by, he cried to the king and said, "Your servant went out into the midst of the battle; and behold, a man turned aside and brought a man to me and said, 'Guard this man; if for any reason he is missing, then your life shall be for his life, or else you shall pay a talent of silver.' And while your servant was busy here and there, he was gone." And the king of Israel said to him, "So shall your judgment be; you yourself have decided it." Then he hastily took the bandage away from his eyes, and the king of Israel recognized him that he was of the prophets. And he said to him, "Thus says the Lord, 'Because you have let go out of your hand the man whom I had devoted to destruction, therefore your life shall go for his life, and your people for his people.'" So the king of Israel went to his house sullen and vexed, and came to Samaria. 1 Kings 20:39-43

Nevertheless, anything which a man sets apart to the Lord out of all that he has, of man or animal or of the fields of his own property, shall not be sold or redeemed. Anything devoted to destruction is most holy to the Lord. Leviticus 27:28

But the people took some of the spoil, sheep and oxen, the choicest of the things devoted to destruction, to sacrifice to the Lord your God at Gilgal. 1saiah 15:21

For My sword is satiated in heaven, Behold it shall descend for judgment upon Edom, And upon the people whom I have devoted to destruction. Isaiah 34:5

God holds the authority to designate or devote. In the battle of Jericho I recently saw that God specifically devoted the silver and gold to Himself and the people of the city were devoted for destruction. Like a parent removing danger from His children's lives, He lovingly removes future temptations, though it doesn't seem so "loving" to us to annihilate an entire city full of people. Where we fall into trouble is when we decide God doesn't know what He's doing, when we decide to hold on to something He has marked for discard and when we put value on something He has marked "dung." I am speaking of things and opportunities here. God never views people as "dung" or marks anyone for destruction. He allows our choices to mark us. Here is a thought, lest we feel sorry for the people of Jericho: any one of them or all of them could have made the same move Rahab did. She recognized the power of God and wanted to align her life with His. She gave up her former "gods" and ways. God received her response of faith and put her in the family tree of the Messiah. We mark ourselves as devoted to God or devoted to destruction by our choices.

So if you are being besieged by the enemy today, take heart. The battlefield is your mind, and you have all authority to make decrees over today's thinking. You are not outnumbered; you are more than a conqueror. You are not under resourced; you are sufficiently supplied. Listen to the Lord for instructions. Read His Word. He will certainly show you the specific strategy to victory. Become mustered and provisioned through prayer. Then, though you look like a flock of goats against a multitude, you will walk away the victor. And when the battle is over and you are riding the chariot of victory, don't become complacent in your decision making and team building. The enemy will surely return at another time to continue the encounter.

<u>Prayer Journal entry:</u>
8/16/05 Yesterday my kids and I went to deliver a meal to a family from church. We saw lots of police cars in the neighborhood we

had just entered. We were told by an officer with a drawn gun to park immediately. Suddenly some Christian friends that we know from some community involvements appeared at our car and pulled us into their home, which is located right at the corner where we had parked. We found out later that an armed man was on a shooting spree right where we were heading. The Lord provided a time of fellowship with our friends and safety for us until the danger had passed. We headed back home with thankful hearts.

Prayer Journal entry:
10/19/05 My computer's hard drive fries with this book two-thirds completed and no back-up files.
10/22/05 Our friend Scott is able to recover all data, but warns me not to trust the computer because it has a serious hard drive error.
11/3/05 The computer is down again. By this time I recognize the blue screen of death. Smile.
11/11/05 After teaching a lesson on Thanksgiving and after a conscious decision to thank the Lord in all circumstances, I try the computer again, and it works! The blue screen momentarily jogs and the Windows screen comes up as normal.
11/14/05 The computer has the blue screen of death again.
11/19/05 The computer works again.
11/20/05 The book is completed in its initial form and completely backed up on my memory key. Praise the Lord!
12/1/05 My brother and sister-in-law give our family a brand new computer and printer.

7

DANCING IN VICTORY

The most wonderful thing about God's promises is: they work! When we rely on Him for His direction in a situation, when we rely on His strength in our weakness, when we choose the road of obedience even when it doesn't look productive or successful, we find victory. And victory is sweet. When we overcome a nagging habit, it is time to dance the dance of victory. When we hold our words in a tense moment of temper, it is time to kick up our heels. When we trust God through the duration of a difficult trial, we have reason to celebrate. We have won a mighty victory!

As I have been reading through the book of Joshua I have seen a wonderful thing: when God's people obey, they are victorious. The Old Testament wanderings of the Israelites show us that grumbling, complaining and misdirected worship will reap us nothing but trouble, but the book of Joshua shows us that trust and attention to God's strategy results in VICTORY. We get a chance, like the Israelites, to put OUR feet on the neck of OUR enemy. *(And it came about when they brought these kings out to Joshua, that Joshua called for all the men of Israel, and said to the chiefs of the men of war who had gone with him, "Come near, put your feet on the necks of these kings." So they came near and put their feet on their necks. Joshua 10:24)* What a feeling!

Today God promises you spiritual victory. Don't confuse this with "success," "riches," or "fame," These are the world's cubic zirconium for the diamond he has in mind for you. He wants you to experience His mighty power working through YOU. God wants you, despite your limitations, to become an overcoming spiritual person who enjoys seeing His power work over, under and through your everyday challenges. Like Joshua, God wants to arm you with today's winning strategy. He wants to see ruts changed, bondages broken and territory taken.

When I first began meditating on chapter six of Joshua, it seemed like God had taken a giant highlighter and emphasized the words TIGHTLY SHUT (verse 1). I could visualize Jericho with its impressive wall, its pompous king and its valiant warriors. By the world's standards it was tightly shut. And for emphasis, we see that NO ONE could go in or out. That's a shut situation, all right. But by the end of the chapter we see that Jericho has been laid wide open. It has become Israel's *possessed* real estate with a giant "sold" sign out front. A pagan woman and her family have been "converted" through faith, and later we see a spiritual legacy built within the family tree of the Messiah Himself. Wow! That's victory.

Are there some areas or lives near you that seem TIGHTLY SHUT off from God's power and work? Is our access for evangelism blocked by someone's "wall?" Then we can learn some lessons from this chapter.

*Now Jericho was **tightly shut** because of the sons of Israel; **no one** went out and **no one** came in. And the Lord said to Joshua, "**See**, I* *have given Jericho into your hand, with its king and the valiant warriors." Joshua 6:1-2*

Although Jericho was fortified like Fort Knox, the Lord wanted Joshua to picture it conquered, and a done deal. I am not encouraging any new age "visualization" techniques here. I am simply pointing out that while the city was sealed in a physical sense, the Lord was pressing Joshua to understand mentally that its huge wall had the potential to be crumbled. Which of us would have believed the day before it actually happened that the Berlin Wall would someday be removed? Who could have visualized that the Soviet Union, which had been one of the most entrenched fortresses against the gospel, would someday eat evangelism up like bread? There is one group of people who I'm sure could picture it: those who had been praying for the country and the minds of its people to open. Here is the point of this chapter: Jesus told His disciples in Matthew 17:20 that NOTHING would be impossible for them if they understood that faith was their ultimate weapon.

*And He said to them, "Because of the littleness of your faith; for truly I say to you, if you have faith as a mustard seed, you shall say to this mountain, 'Move from here to there,' and it shall move; **and nothing shall be impossible to you**." Matthew 17:20*

And you shall march around the city, all the men of war circling the city once. You shall do so for six days. Also seven priests shall carry seven trumpets of rams' horns before the ark; then on the seventh day you shall march around the city seven times, and the priests shall blow the trumpets. And it shall be that when they make a long blast with the ram's horn, and when you hear the sound of the trumpet, all the people shall shout with a great shout;

and the wall of the city will fall down flat, and the people will go up every man straight ahead. Joshua 6:3-5

At the end of Joshua chapter 5, we read about Joshua's encounter with the Captain of the Host. He had a face-to-face encounter with the Lord. We all know that verse and chapter markings were added much later to the text of Scripture and sometimes I think they get in the way of the message of the Word. In this case Joshua had a mighty encounter with the presence of God Almighty and, without a break in thought, we are led to picture a seemingly impossible battle where trumpets bring down a wall thick enough for chariots to ride across. This small section is absolutely essential to the victory of Jericho, for if we can see that our battle is God's will, we have the victory we desire within our grasp. Joshua had an incredible worship experience of seeing the sword of the Lord drawn. From that point on his only worry was to follow through on instructions, for he knew the Lord would fight for them. Their weapons could be feathers (or trumpets) and they would succeed. Is the thing you are asking of the Lord lined up with His will? Is He fighting for you in this arena? Then prepare for victory. It won't elude you.

Now it came about when Joshua was by Jericho, that he lifted up his eyes and looked, and behold, a man was standing opposite him with his sword drawn in his hand, and Joshua went to him and said to him, "Are you for us or for our adversaries?" And he said, "No, rather I indeed come now as captain of the host of the Lord." And Joshua fell on his face to the earth, and bowed down, and said to him, "What has my lord to say to his servant?" And the captain of the Lord's host said to Joshua, "Remove your sandals from your feet, for the place where you are standing is holy." And Joshua did so. Joshua 5:13-15

Here is an essential truth in obtaining our victories: our part is authentic, profound worship of the Most High God. The captain of the Lord, when honored and adored, picks up the sword that conquers the enemy. His part is the actual battle.

I used to think that the priests in this story just blew their trumpets one time each day. I got that idea from the from many Sunday School teachers who had us act out the story as children and from the phrase that talks about the one long blast right before the people shouted and the wall fell down. But now as I study verse nine and thirteen, I picture the priests in more of a continual state of worship. The people weren't talking during their march. They weren't singing. But perhaps they were meditating on the goodness of God. I wonder what the trumpeters played on those seven marches around the city. Perhaps the trumpeters were playing a worship song, like A Mighty Fortress is Our God, or the Jewish equivalent. Smile. The point is that worship is key in our victory over any situation. We are not capable in our own ability to bring down a wall, physical or mental. But our adoration of the Captain of the Host prompts Him to act on our behalf.

And the armed men went before the priests who blew the trumpets, and the rear guard came after the ark, while they **continued to blow the trumpets**. *Joshua 6:9*

And the seven priests carrying the seven trumpets of rams' horns before the ark of the Lord went on **continually, and blew the trumpets**; *and the armed men went before them, and the rear guard came after the ark of the Lord, while they* **continued to blow the trumpets**. *Joshua 6:13*

So Joshua the son of Nun called the priests and said to them, "Take up the Ark of the Covenant, and let seven priests carry seven trumpets of rams' horns before the ark of the Lord." Then he *said to the people, "Go forward, and march around the city, and let the armed men go on before the ark of the Lord." And it was so, that when Joshua had spoken to the people, the seven priests carrying the seven trumpets of rams' horns before the Lord went forward and blew the trumpets; and the ark of the covenant of the Lord followed them. And the armed men went before the priests who blew the trumpets, and the **rear guard** came after the ark, while they continued to blow the trumpets. But Joshua commanded the people, saying, "You shall not shout nor let your voice be heard, nor let a word proceed out of your mouth, **until the day I tell you, 'Shout!' Then you shall shout!**" Joshua 6:6-10*

     Take up the presence of God (represented by the Ark of the Covenant), follow God's commands carefully and when I tell you to, SHOUT. All three of these instructions are critical to victory: we must be saturated in the presence of the Lord, we must be obedient to what the Lord tells us to do and we must respond in faith to what the Lord asks us to believe Him for.

     Why must we be in His presence? Because relationship with Jesus will correct wrong behaviors, motives and plans. The Lord and His Word can draw out why we are doing something; it can expose the hidden motives.

For the word of God is living and active and sharper than any two-edged sword, and piercing as far as the division of soul and spirit, of both joints and marrow, and able to judge the thoughts and intentions of the heart. Hebrews 4:12

     Why must we be obedient? Because we don't have the wisdom to understand the "why" of God's plan. Who could have figured out that the way into the city of Jericho was to walk around it? Who would have thought that a shout was better than a demolition ball and crane? We aren't capable of figuring out the "how to"s in God's workshop. We do best when we simply follow orders and complete the tasks we have been given.

Why must we SHOUT? It's interesting to me that when the Israelites were told to shout, there was nothing yet to shout about. They were to shout a victory cry when there was yet no victory. The shout came before the wall fell, and yet the shout was crucial to the wall actually falling. The shout represents the faith we need to accomplish great things for God. He wants us to learn to celebrate the victory long before it is realized.

So he had the ark of the Lord taken around the city, circling it once; then they came into the camp and spent the night in the camp. Now Joshua rose early in the morning, and the priests took up the ark of the Lord. And the seven priests carrying the seven trumpets of rams' horns before the ark of the Lord went on continually, and blew the trumpets; and the armed men went before them, **and the rear guard came after the ark of the Lord***, while they continued to blow the trumpets. Thus the second day they marched around the city once and returned to the camp; they did so for six days. Then it came about on the seventh day that they rose early at the dawning of the day and marched around the city in the same manner seven times; only on that day they marched around the city seven times. And it came about at the seventh time, when the priests blew the trumpets, Joshua said to the people, "Shout! For the Lord has given you the city." Joshua 6:1-16*

The Lord gives directions for a "rear guard" in this faith adventure. Whenever we are trying to acquire new territory or break open a closed one it is an important principle to learn that offensive prayer must be backed up with defensive prayer. I have only learned this through experience. My friend Kathy, of the ministry *Heavenly Treasures*, goes into nations that are deeply infested demonic territories. She found she needed a prayer shield of people covering her and her family as she attempted to open up strongholds of the enemy's influence. In a similar way, when our church is trying to open up new areas of ministry, we need to pray over unity and harmony or we see a backlash from our efforts.

And the city shall be under the ban, it and all that is in it belongs to the Lord; only Rahab the harlot and all who are with her in the house shall live, because she hid the messengers whom we sent. But as for you, only keep yourselves from the things under the ban, lest you covet them and take some of the things under the ban, so you would make the camp of Israel accursed and bring trouble on it. But all the silver and gold and articles of bronze and iron are holy to the Lord; they shall go into the treasury of the Lord. Joshua 6:17

      I have always felt a little sorry for Achan. Being stoned to death with your entire family had always seemed a little harsh until the Holy Spirit pressed onto my heart what he actually did. God had designated everything in the city as an offering to Himself. He had proclaimed it sacred and set apart for His own treasuries. This sacred consecration was made known to the entire nation of Israel before the battle. Yet Achan snubbed God's holy plan and coveted items for himself. It was a kick in the face at best. God did not have a history of unrealistic demands. He had shown Joshua in chapter five who was going to win the battle: He was. The spoil belonged to him because he had fought for it. Had the Israelites battled? No. They had simply walked and shouted.

So the people shouted, and priests blew the trumpets; and it came about, when the people heard the sound of the trumpet, that the people shouted with a great shout and the wall fell down flat, so that the people went up into the city, every man straight ahead, and they took the city. And they utterly destroyed everything in the city, both man and woman, young and old, and ox and sheep and donkey, with the edge of the sword. And Joshua said to the two men who had spied out the land, "Go into the harlot's house and bring the woman and all she has out of there, as you have sworn to her." So the young men who were spies went in and brought out Rahab and her father and her mother and her brothers and all she had; they also brought out all her relatives, and placed them outside the camp of Israel. And they burned the city with fire, and all that was in it. Only the silver and gold and articles of bronze and iron, they put into the treasury of the house of the Lord. However, Rahab the harlot and her father's household and all she had, Joshua spared; and she has lived in the midst of Israel to this day, for she hid the messengers whom Joshua sent to spy out Jericho. Then Joshua made them take an oath at that time, saying, "Cursed before the Lord is the man who rises up and builds this city Jericho; with the loss of his first-born he shall lay its foundation, and with the loss of his youngest son he shall set up its gates." So the Lord was with Joshua, and his fame was in all the land. Joshua 6:20-27

The prize for obedience is changed lives. Because Joshua obeyed God, a former harlot became a believer and the generations that followed her did too. Former pagans were now worshipping as a result of obedient people putting one foot in front of the other, just as God had commanded. For those in the front lines of ministry, this is a very important prize on which to keep our eyes. Why do we do what we do? We share the gospel of Christ and take hits doing it because, through our God, harlots can become saints. The enemy wants us to think that "walking around the city" day after day is futile. He wants us to focus on the incredibly bizarre weapons of trumpets and stop the parade. He wants us to see sealed cities with political and military forces that say this place is off limits for the people of God and His marvelous message. But no matter where we are looking, no matter how deeply entrenched the enemy is, we must remember our unforgettable encounter with the Captain of the Host, His Sword and that He has said "nothing is impossible" for us.

Prayer Journal entry:
After my computer hard drive crashed and while it was being looked at for repair, I realized that I had no contact information for an upcoming speaking engagement without my Outlook program. I only knew the woman's first name, Val, and the city, Littlerock, California.
On 10/22/05 I pleaded with the Lord to have her call me or something. I reminded Him that He had authorized this speaking engagement and had given me a message to share. I found out later that day that my computer had been repaired. The first thing I did after receiving it back was to print all the contact information for this event, which was held on 11/06/05. Thank you Lord!

Prayer Journal entry:
July '05 Made a commitment to play the harp at a wedding in September. I have been assured that I can play with another musician so there won't be a lot of pressure to play "solo." I am working on rehearsing for another event in September and spend most of my time working on that music.
9/21/05 Found out that, like it or not, I am playing <u>all alone</u> for this wedding. It is being held outside and there isn't a piano or even the means to set one up. There is not much time to prepare and I ask the Lord for His help.
9/23/05 Realize I need to record a piano CD that I can play with if I am going to be able to pull this off. My friend Leon makes time to record one with me on Thursday.

9/28/05 The Lord definitely helps this limited musician on the day of the wedding. I know in my heart that without His help it would have been a disaster.

Prayer Journal entry:
Two of my husband's friends are a Messianic Rabbi named Joseph Hilbrant and a Jordanian Christian named Ameal Haddad. He knew they should meet each other. This was not easy to accomplish. Each was suspicious of the other and it took lots of time to build a friendship and trust.
10/22/05 We visited a special service at Rabbi Joseph's Jewish-Christian Unity Congregation. Rabbi Joseph had Pastor Ameal bring the message. Only in the body of Christ could a Jew and an Arab worship in peace. Praise the Lord!

8

DANCING IN THANKFULNESS

I write a lot of thank you notes. That's because we have a wonderful congregation full of loving, helpful people. Recently, after a special event at our church, I found myself writing over thirty notes! It made me wonder how the president keeps up with all his thank you notes. Does he have professional "thankers" on his staff? Do people show up at the White House with only one task on their minds: to spend their days thanking those who have shown kindness to him and his office?

It used to be that we had pastoral titles that were plain and ordinary. You either had a pastor or a youth pastor. But nowadays we have very creative titles: Pastor of Helps, Pastor of Evangelism, even Pastor of Multi-Media. Smile. But how about hiring a full-time pastor to just come to work and thank the Lord everyday for His goodness. Does that sound eccentric?

David was a man who understood the power of thankfulness. He knew that his success came from the Lord. Everyday he wanted to note the kindness and graciousness of the

Lord, so he appointed professional "thankers." He selected a man by the name of Asaph, along with his relatives, for the purpose of thanking God morning and evening.

How did they do their job? Sometimes they thanked Him with cymbals, sometimes with trumpets, sometimes they sang, and sometimes they prophesied, but they were to concentrate on thanking the Lord every day of their lives. It was their calling. They were to talk of all His wondrous works.

Asaph and his relatives were appointed by name to this task. It was at the top of their "to do" list each day. But do you and I see ourselves in the role of professional "thankers?" Do we consider that we have been appointed as well (by name) for this same precious privilege?

I have noticed that when I read our church's update for prayer requests and praises, I am drawn to pray for needs, but sometimes I mentally check off and skip the praises. It's just easier to ask than it is to thank. Sometimes we even talk to others about the good things God has done, but we forget to actually thank *Him*. Have you ever been grateful for a gift, but never sent a thank you card? There are times we even tell others how much we appreciate a gift, but forget to tell the person that blessed us how thankful we are. We could use some tips from these professional "thankers."

They were designated by name to give thanks both morning and evening.

*With them were Heman and Jeduthun, and the rest who were chosen, who were **designated by name**, to give thanks to the Lord, because His lovingkindness is everlasting. 1 Chronicles 16:41*

*So he left Asaph and his relatives there before the ark of the covenant of the Lord to minister before the ark continually, **as every day's work required**. 1 Chronicles 16:37*

*They are to stand **every morning** to thank and to praise the Lord, and likewise at **evening**. 1 Chronicles. 23:30*

They weren't left all alone in this responsibility. David was constantly writing new psalms to give them words to sing and pray. He saw himself in the role of "thanker" also. We can see this by the huge amount of his writings that were devoted to praise and thanksgiving.

Then on that day David first assigned Asaph and his relatives to give thanks to the Lord. Oh give thanks to the Lord, call upon His name; make known His deeds among the peoples. Sing to Him, sing praises to Him; speak of all His wonders. 1 Chronicles 16:7-9

Thanksgiving is a powerful weapon. It is like praise in that way. Praise is our response for who God is. Thanksgiving is our response for what He's done.

Read over this passage and then we will take at a look at the truths it gives us.

Now it came about after this that the sons of Moab and the sons of Ammon, together with some of the Meunites, came to make war against Jehoshaphat. Then some came and reported to Jehoshaphat, saying, "A great multitude is coming against you from beyond the sea, out of Aram and behold, they are in Hazazon-tamar (that is Engedi)." **Jehoshaphat was afraid** and **turned his attention to seek the Lord**, *and proclaimed a fast throughout all Judah. So Judah gathered together* **to seek help from the Lord**; *they even came from all the cities of Judah to seek the Lord.* **Then Jehoshaphat stood in the assembly of Judah and Jerusalem, in the house of the Lord before the new court, and he said, "O Lord, the God of our fathers, are You not God in the heavens? And are You** *not ruler over all the kingdoms of the nations? Power* *and might are in Your hand so that no one can stand against You. Did You not, O our God, drive out the inhabitants of this land before Your people Israel and give it to the descendants of Abraham Your friend forever? They have lived in it, and have built You a sanctuary there for Your name, saying,* **"Should evil come upon us, the sword, or judgment, or pestilence, or famine, we will stand before this house and before You (for Your name is in this house) and cry to You in our distress, and You will hear and deliver us.'** *Now behold, the sons of Ammon and Moab and Mount Seir, whom You did not let Israel invade when they came out of the land of Egypt (they turned aside from them and did not destroy them), see how they are rewarding us by coming to drive us out from Your possession which You have given us as an inheritance. O our God, will You not judge them? For* **we are powerless before this great multitude who are coming against us; nor do we know what to do, but our eyes are on You.**" *All Judah was standing before the Lord, with their infants, their wives and their children. Then in the midst of the assembly the Spirit of the Lord came upon Jahaziel the son of Zechariah, the son of Benaiah, the son of Jeiel, the son of Mattaniah, the Levite of the sons of Asaph; and he said, "Listen, all Judah and the inhabitants of Jerusalem and King Jehoshaphat: thus says the Lord to you, 'Do not fear or be dismayed because of this great multitude, for the battle is not yours but God's. Tomorrow go down against them. Behold, they will come up by the ascent of Ziz, and you will find them at the end of the valley in front of the wilderness of Jeruel. You need not fight in this battle; station yourselves, stand and see the salvation of the Lord on your behalf, O Judah and Jerusalem.' Do not fear or be dismayed; tomorrow go out to face them, for the Lord is with you."* **Jehoshaphat bowed his head with his face to the ground, and all Judah and the inhabitants of Jerusalem fell down before the Lord, worshiping the Lord.** *The Levites, from the sons of the Kohathites and of the sons of the Korahites, stood up to praise the*

Lord God of Israel, with a very loud voice. They rose early in the morning and went out to the wilderness of Tekoa; and when they went out, Jehoshaphat stood and said, "Listen to me, O Judah and inhabitants of Jerusalem, put your trust in the Lord your God and you will be established. Put your trust in His prophets and succeed." When he had consulted with the people, he appointed those who sang to the Lord and those who praised Him in holy attire, as they went out before the army and said, **"Give thanks to the Lord, for His loving-kindness is everlasting." When they began singing and praising, the Lord set ambushes** against the sons of Ammon, Moab and Mount Seir, who had come against Judah; so they were routed. For the sons of Ammon and Moab rose up against the inhabitants of Mount Seir destroying them completely; and when they had finished with the inhabitants of Seir, they helped to destroy one another. When Judah came to the lookout of the wilderness, they looked toward the multitude, and behold, they were corpses lying on the ground, and no one had escaped. When Jehoshaphat and his people came to take their spoil, they found much among them, including goods, garments and valuable things which they took for themselves, more than they could carry. And they were three days taking the spoil because there was so much. 2 Chronicles Chapter 20

There was a multitude coming.

King Jehosaphat had received word that a huge army was coming against him. This army was comprised of the Ammorites, the Moabites and the Meunites. The army was totally overwhelming and Jehosaphat became afraid. Perhaps you can relate. Have there been some days where you got a word like the one Jehosaphat received? When no matter how you tried to look beyond the circumstances you found yourself also feeling afraid and running for cover? Thank goodness Jehosaphat knew where to take his troubles. He took them to the Lord.

<u>They didn't know what to do.</u>
     He gathered all of Judah to fast and pray, but they certainly didn't seem to have any answers. Jehosaphat made an incredible statement in the middle of this critical time of worship: *"We don't know what to do Lord, but our eyes are on your, Lord."* What a statement this is! Oh if we could only come to the Lord in the middle of each crisis WE encounter and say this very thing to the Lord.

<u>The prophet gave the message that the battle was His, but they had to internalize and believe it.</u>
     In the middle of this incredible corporate worship time, the Lord sent a message to His people through the prophet, Jahaziel.

Then in the midst of the assembly the Spirit of the Lord came upon Jahaziel the son of Zechariah, the son of Benaiah, the son of Jeiel, the son of Mattaniah, the Levite of the sons of Asaph; and he said, "Listen, all Judah and the inhabitants of Jerusalem and King Jehoshaphat: thus says the Lord to you, 'Do not fear or be dismayed because of this great multitude, for the battle is not yours but God's. Tomorrow go down against them. Behold, they will come up by the ascent of Ziz, and you will find them at the end of the valley in front of the wilderness of Jeruel. You need not fight in this battle; station yourselves, stand and see the salvation of the Lord on your behalf, O Judah and Jerusalem.' Do not fear or be dismayed; tomorrow go out to face them, for the Lord is with you."
2 Chronicles 20:14-17

     Its one thing for God to send us a message of reassurance, but it's quite another thing for us to believe it. This particular message said in effect, "Don't worry, it's His problem to bring the victory, not yours." Again and again in my own life's circumstances, the Lord has issued this decree through His written Word. Many times I have internalized the truth and walked onto the battlefield armed with peace. Other times I have merely paced back and forth in a tizzy, wondering if He could be trusted.

I am so glad that the Israelites "got it" on this particular day. It began in the king's heart. He believed the Word of God and he bowed and worshipped. But then everyone began to seize the fact that victory was coming and it had nothing to do with their skill in battle, their tremendous resources or strategies. It was coming because of God's faithfulness to His people.

Young pastors are funny at times. Some come and see our beautiful church buildings and see people praying and ask dumb questions like, "How did YOU do it?" Because time and time again we have stood in Jehosaphat's shoes and watched the multitude coming, heard the still small voice calm our hearts and walked into battle armed with a song, it is obvious to us HOW the battle was won. It has nothing to do with who we are and everything to do with who He is. We know what it is like to walk in the midst of overwhelming weakness into a battle where the victory has been determined by the Lord's premeditated grace.

The singers had to believe the Word or they would have never been able to sing while facing swords, spears and slingshots. Their thankful hearts were their weapons that day.

In order to walk into the battle and face real swords and real spears, to face angry enemies by the thousands, you have to really "get" the message. You have to internalize that the battle is the Lord's.

To realize how powerful our thankfulness is becomes a weapon in itself. To realize how much God longs to hear the gratitude of His people and how pleased He is that we have noticed His care becomes equipment in the Christian life that cannot be diminished.

It was while working on this particular lesson I had that interesting trial of my computer's hard drive crashing. One day I had an error message and tried to reboot. Things didn't go as usual and instead of the lovely Windows screen, I was facing the BLUE SCREEN OF DEATH. I waited sometimes patiently and sometimes not while different computer technicians looked at it. I thought about the book you are reading right now that was locked behind that blue screen of death, and I wondered if the lessons logged in on it would ever be recovered.

Then one night, I got word that all my data had been retrieved. What a blessed night of thanksgiving that was! I received the computer back with a warning: "Do not trust your hard drive. It has a serious error and the crash is bound to happen again." A week later it did crash again. However, I had already learned a valuable lesson. There is life without a computer. Honestly, this was an important lesson to learn in this day and age. The Lord used the time I couldn't be on the computer to return me to other forms of communications: the phone, the fax machine and finally the handwritten letter. All were effective and God used them during my time of waiting.

So when the computer crashed the second time it wasn't quite so devastating. As wonderful as God's timing is, I was supposed to present a lesson on thanksgiving right after the second crash. I was relating to the people raising their voices and saying, "Give thanks to the Lord!" So conscientiously I began thanking Him from that point on. I thanked him for saved data, I thanked Him for being bigger than a computer and I thanked Him for always providing what I need. The next night I had a little thought about reconnecting the computer and trying it out. At first I got the blue screen of death and then, as if someone had punched a button, the computer went into its normal startup mode and was back.

A computer is not as life-threatening as a battle (unless you're a writer like me), but perhaps you can relate with a battle of your own. Have you employed the tool of thanksgiving? Have you internalized the message given to you by the Lord and are you ready to walk into whatever circumstances He will lead you through?

<u>As they began to sing, "O give thanks unto the Lord…" the Lord set ambushes against the enemy.</u>
        This is the good part. As they thanked the Lord for his faithfulness, and as the notes of their song rose into Heaven's ears, the Lord set ambushes for the enemy. It was like when Paul and Silas began singing in prison and the earthquake happened that opened their prison gates. When we thank Him for His care He can set ambushes for the enemy because He knows what will trip him up. In this passage, they began killing each other. Ha! I love that. The enemy wiped out the enemy. I like to picture me thanking the Lord for His goodness and the proponents of abortion destroying each other. We can have the dealers of drugs, pornography and homosexuality turn on themselves with defeating tactics while we sing and praise and meditate on God's goodness. It's a delightful strategy.
        What had looked like God's anger was actually God's favor because He had intended them to receive three days full of plunder (not destruction).
        When the word came that the multitude was on the march, I'll bet the Israelites didn't feel very blessed. They might have thought things like this: Do you love us, God? Have we offended you? Why have you allowed this terrible tragedy? They couldn't see that from God's perspective He was trying to give them three days of plunder for free with no effort involved whatsoever. The very thing that looked like disfavor to them was really an opportunity for growth, prosperity and blessing. Many times it is adversity that opens up the resource of thanksgiving.

Trials actually assist in increasing our thankfulness. When things are going great, do we thank God more? No. Unfortunately when food is plentiful we aren't as thankful as when we've gone without.

One year at Azusa Pacific University I ministered in Mexico with some other students over the Thanksgiving break. On Thanksgiving Day the ovens broke down and we ended up eating peanut butter and jelly sandwiches for our holiday meal. I was lonely. I missed my family. I missed eating turkey and I missed my warm bed. However, this particular trial produced a huge harvest of thanksgiving in my life. Every year when I sit down now for a Thanksgiving meal I am SO GLAD that I am not in Mexico, that I am not eating peanut butter and jelly sandwiches and that I am with my loved ones. I can almost hardly contain my gratitude.

It becomes a continuous cycle of thanksgiving God allows trials, we cry out for His help, He answers and supplies, and our thankfulness grows to new heights.

Now He who supplies seed to the sower and bread for food will supply and multiply your seed for sowing and increase the harvest of your righteousness; you will be enriched in everything for all liberality, which through us is producing thanksgiving to God. For the ministry of this service is not only fully supplying the needs of the saints, but is also overflowing through many thanksgivings to God. Because of the proof given by this ministry, they will glorify God for your obedience to your confession of the gospel of Christ and for the liberality of your contribution to them and to all, while they also, by prayer on your behalf, yearn for you because of the surpassing grace of God in you. **Thanks be to God for His indescribable gift!** *2 Corinthians 9:10-15*

We are to:
Thank Him completely - Psalm 9:1

Thank Him willingly - Psalm 54:6
Thank Him continually - Hebrews 13:15
Thank Him to the next generation - Isaiah 38:19
Thank Him for others - 1 Corinthians 1:14 and Ephesians 1:16
Thank Him for all things and circumstances - Ephesians 5:20, 1 Thessalonians 5:18 and Philippians 1:12, 4:13

<u>The enemy likes to use our pride to keep us from expressing thankfulness.</u>
    The enemy hates a thankful heart so he does his best to get us to shut up about God's faithfulness. I was in a service shortly after the Lord had helped recover all my computer data and heard someone ask the question, "Does anyone have a praise to share tonight?" I thought of my praise, but immediately a conversation began in my mind. The enemy said, "You talk too much at these services. No one cares about your little computer anyway." Satan's talk was hushed by the expression of my grateful heart. Perhaps you have experienced times when the enemy tried to keep you silent over the goodness of the Lord. .
    Here are some verses from our friend, David, to help us with actually writing God some well deserved thank you notes and to help us see the importance of expressing our thanksgiving in the presence of others:

I will give thanks to the Lord according to His righteousness, and will sing praise to the name of the Lord Most High. Psalm 7:17

(For the choir director; on Muth-labben. A Psalm of David.) I will give thanks to the Lord with all my heart; I will tell of all Thy wonders. Psalm 9:1

Therefore I will give thanks to Thee among the nations, O Lord, and I will sing praises to Thy name. Psalm 18:49

Sing praise to the Lord, you His godly ones, and give thanks to His holy name. Psalm 30:4

That my soul may sing praise to Thee, and not be silent. O Lord my God, I will give thanks to Thee forever. Psalm 30:12

Give thanks to the Lord with the lyre; Sing praises to Him with a harp of ten strings. Psalm 33:2

I will give Thee thanks in the great congregation; I will praise Thee among a mighty throng. Psalm 35:18

In God we have boasted all day long, and we will give thanks to Thy name forever. Selah. Psalm 44:8

I will cause Thy name to be remembered in all generations; therefore the peoples will give Thee thanks forever and ever. Psalm 45:17

I will give Thee thanks forever, because Thou hast done it, and I will wait on Thy name, for it is good, in the presence of Thy godly ones. Psalm 52:9

Willingly I will sacrifice to Thee; I will give thanks to Thy name, O Lord, for it is good. Psalm 54:6

I will give thanks to Thee, O Lord, among the peoples; I will sing praises to Thee among the nations. Psalm 57:9

So we Thy people and the sheep of Thy pasture will give thanks to Thee forever; to all generations we will tell of Thy praise. Psalm 79:13

Be glad in the Lord, you righteous ones; and give thanks to His holy name. Psalm 97:12

Enter His gates with thanksgiving, And His courts with praise. Give thanks to Him; bless His name. Psalm 100:4

Oh give thanks to the Lord, call upon His name; Make known His deeds among the peoples. Psalm 105:1

Praise the Lord! Oh give thanks to the Lord, for He is good; For His lovingkindness is everlasting. Psalm 106:1

Prayer Journal entry:
8/10/04 I was asked by my friend to pray for four friends of hers who had been hurt in a ministry situation. They have visited our church occasionally, but they are just names to me now.
11/05 All four are now serving in our church!

Prayer Journal entry:
11/09/05 Woke up late for my quiet time. Usually the Lord wakes me up in time to have two hours with Him before I have to get ready, but this morning I only had one hour. This is very unusual. During the time I did have to pray and read the Word, the enemy reminded me, by planting a little thought in my head, that I needed to make a dessert for our Bible study brunch that morning. I hadn't been able to make it the night before because I was leading a meeting, which had required all-day preparation. I decided that my time with Him was more important than looking organized to my Bible study friends. After my quiet time was over it was 7 a.m. and we have to leave the house by 8:15 a.m. I needed to dress as well as get the kids ready for school. The Lord quickened my mind to grab two cans of cherries and a recipe. A cherry crisp baked while

I got ready. By 8:15 we were all ready AND the dessert was also made. When I got to corporate prayer time at the church, the enemy reminded me that I needed to make copies of music for the worship team I was leading that night. I decided to go to prayer and figure out later what to do about the music. I went from corporate prayer straight to the brunch. After the brunch my friend Michelle asked if I needed help with anything. I asked her if she could copy the music. She did. I was able to prepare the missions fundraiser caramel apples on time (by 3 p.m.), to lead worship and to teach on thankfulness that night. How glad I am that the Lord rewards our decisions to trust and honor Him.

Conclusion

This world system intends to stomp out the dance of your prayer. Yet whether we are facing famine, dire conflict, the flames of persecution or the slow besiegement of our enemy, we can find joy in turning our plodding steps into a little jig of praise and thanksgiving. We can dance in the fire because He is there with us. We can leap over the waves because He reaches out His hand. We can believe that He can save us FROM our circumstances. We can believe that He can save us IN our circumstances. We can focus on the thought that He will save us from this trial and we can focus on the thought that He will save us IN this trial. But even if for some reason He chooses not to save us in the way we believe He should, we can be sure that dancing on the hot coals of our circumstances will only bring Him honor. It may be just a warm-up for the final and endless ballroom dance of blessing up ahead.

So celebrate today. Your trials are producing a great impact on the world around you whether you can see it or not. The Lord sees the big picture of your life, and your decisions to faithfully intercede will lead to destinations of blessing. There are no wrong turns with trust. Through each and every circumstance that your prayers take you, there will be dances of answered prayer as wonderful as the one Miriam danced after the Red Sea had been parted. Just as she never forgot her dance, you will never be able to forget the times God has asked you to lead the dance of faithful praying for others and saw him do mighty things. You will remember with wonder His initial tapping on your shoulder.

He comes each day with an invitation for you to dance. Will He find you at the window? Will he find you willing to waltz where you cannot see? Will he find you waiting with a heart of thanksgiving in the midst of your furnace or prison? Will you take the hand He offers so that the limits of earthly living will bind you no longer and you will begin to soar, feet barely touching, into the realm where no barriers to human understanding exist. This is the place He referred to when he told the disciples in Matthew 17:20b *"...and nothing shall be impossible to you."*

www.ingramcontent.com/pod-product-compliance
Lightning Source LLC
Chambersburg PA
CBHW032053150426
43194CB00006B/515